#whysage   #whyfennel   #whyjuniper   #whyoliveleaf   #whymeadowsweet

#whybasil   #whythyme   #whyrosemary   #   t

№1
BOTANICALS

Available from www.no1botanicals.com

Life is about how far we're moved,
not how far we travel.

Soneva

Rare life

MALDIVES | THAILAND

For reservations contact: 0 800 048 8044 (UK Toll-free number)

New.

Dramatically Different™ Hydrating Jelly
Anti-Pollution

Pure genius.
24-hour hydration repair + pollution protection.

Makes skin 87% less vulnerable to pollution.[*]
Locks in the good, like moisture, and filters out the bad, thanks to Clean Shield Technology.™ Skin is healthy, stronger with a clean glow. No parabens. No phthalates. No fragrance. Just happy skin.

CLINIQUE

Allergy Tested. 100% Fragrance Free.

Contents

The Pioneer Issue

———

Arctic wildernesses. Evolving cities. Remote islands. To mark our 25th issue we went in search of the ideas, destinations and individuals that are changing the way we travel.

STATE OF THE NATION | P. 56
WASHINGTON DC, *USA*

Uncovering the people behind the politics in America's capital against a backdrop of activism and cultural change

TREASURE ISLAND | P. 88
MADAGASCAR

Sugared-almond skies, gargantuan shells and mischievous children bewitch our Digital Editor-in-Chief

MIGHT AND MAGIC | P. 116
BANDA ISLANDS, *INDONESIA*

Sailing through nutmeg-scented islands on a traditional phinisi yacht brings both adventure and a sense of peace

LONG DAY'S JOURNEY INTO NIGHT | P. 140
SVALBARD, *NORWAY*

Our Print Editor-in-Chief confronts the disorienting scale and isolation of this rugged Arctic archipelago

CONTENTS

36
SILENCE IS GOLDEN
UMBRIA, *ITALY*

Rediscovering the value of quiet at a
hillside monastic retreat

––––––

40
SKIN DEEP
ALTEA, *SPAIN*

A full body-and-mind MOT triggers an
emotional transformation

––––––

72
HOPE AND HOMECOMING
BEIRUT, *LEBANON*

Nostalgia for its 1970s heyday is driving a
wave of change in the capital

––––––

80
ONLY CONNECT
GLOBAL

Locating the humanity in the headlines
with the photographer Steve McCurry

––––––

102
GIN AND CROCODILES
MALAWI

Several sachets of Malawi Gin jump-start
an adventure across lake and forest

––––––

108
ABOVE AND BEYOND
KWAZULU-NATAL, *SOUTH AFRICA*

An immersive conservation experience
reveals the faces on the frontline

––––––

126
THE SHAPE OF WATER
GLOBAL

Ocean anecdotes from the champion
freediver Hanli Prinsloo

––––––

134
PASTURES NEW
SØRØYA, *NORWAY*

Joining the indigenous Sami tribe at the
start of the winter reindeer migration

––––––

156
HIGHER GROUND
GLOBAL

The photographer Chris Burkard on how
to protect the Earth's truly wild spaces

––––––

SVALBARD, *NORWAY*

SUITCASE

MEDIA

Behind every brand is a story.
Tell yours.

SOCIAL MEDIA	CREATIVE STRATEGY	BRANDING
BRAND PUBLISHING	PHOTOGRAPHY	WEB DESIGN
COPYWRITING	CONTENT STRATEGY	VIDEOGRAPHY

A FULL-SERVICE AGENCY
HELLO@SUITCASEMEDIA.COM

SUITCASE
MAGAZINE

Founder and CEO
Serena Guen

CREATIVE

Creative Director
Sebastian Bland

Fashion Director
Tona Stell

Designer
Jacob Elwood

INTERNS

Annabel Nugent • Emily Paul
Esme Lear • Kati Brunk
Khadeeja Saleem • Olivia Morelli
Sophia Macpherson • Sophie Inkester
Sylvia Chuku

CONTACT US

Connaught House, 1-3 Mount St,
London, W1K 3NB
hello@SUITCASEmag.com
+44 (0)20 3642 5266

EDITORIAL

Print Editor-in-Chief
Olivia Squire

Sub-Editor
Sarah Frank

Executive Assistant to CEO
Rowena Matterson

SUITCASE
MEDIA

*A content, photography and design agency
focused on travel and lifestyle brands*
hello@SUITCASEmedia.com

Head of Content and Strategy
Alice Leahy
alice@SUITCASEmedia.com

Media Editor
Rae Boocock

Social Media Strategist
Lucinda Bounsall

Director
Moose Guen

DIGITAL

Digital Editor-in-Chief
India Dowley

Head of Digital
Sarah Bentley

Deputy Digital Editor
Gilly Hopper

Contributing Editors
Haley Crawford
Fleur Rollet-Manus

ADVERTISING

Commercial Director
Linda Blank
linda@SUITCASEmag.com

Head of Partnerships
Anna Burbidge
anna@SUITCASEmag.com

DISCOVER MORE
SUITCASEmag.com

@SUITCASEmag   /SUITCASEmagazine   @SUITCASE

Printed in the UK by CPI Colour
Distributed by Pineapple Media Ltd: pineapple-media.com

ALEX BOX | P. 22

The make-up artist and former creative director of the beauty brand Illamasqua, Alex Box, is well-known for her ability to blend the borders between fashion, art and technology, having previously worked for clients including Lady Gaga and Gareth Pugh. She opens her trailblazing toolbox for our Pioneer Beauty Edit.

OTEGHA UWAGBA | P. 68

Otegha Uwagba is the founder of the London-based community Women Who, as well as the author of the best-selling Little Black Book: A Toolkit for Working Women. She explores the latest co-working and co-living concepts aiming to capture the hearts of nomadic millennials worldwide.

STEVE MCCURRY | P. 80

For four decades the photographer Steve McCurry has immersed himself in conflict zones and remote countries around the world in order to portray the shared humanity of cultures. He shows a few of the arresting images captured along the way and answers our questions about his genre-defining work.

HANLI PRINSLOO | P. 126

The champion freediver Hanli Prinsloo is the founder of the I AM WATER Ocean Conservation Foundation along with her partner, Peter Marshall. Together they run ocean experiences for schoolchildren in South Africa as well as freediving trips for travellers in destinations including Mozambique and Mexico. She recollects a few memories from beneath the waves.

BENJAMIN HARDMAN | P. 140

The Australian native Benjamin Hardman embarked on his first photographic mission in an Arctic climate five years ago. His passion for the cold has since led him in search of the North's colossal ice structures, volcanic mountains and resilient wildlife, as he documents on our polar safari in the northerly Norwegian archipelago of Svalbard.

CHRIS BURKARD | P. 156

The photographer Chris Burkard began his career documenting surf culture but has since carved out a niche for himself exploring the most remote regions of the Earth, inspiring humans to consider their relationship with nature and be moved to protect it. He speaks to us about the importance of preserving such wild places and showcases some of his iconic images.

Abbi Kemp • Abigail Lowe • Anna Hart • Aron Klein • Bex Hughes • Billy Bolton • Carly Smith • Chidera Eggerue • Crille Rask Dominic Squire • Dervla Louli • Eduardo Cerruti • George House • Holly Tuppen • Imogen Lepere • James Davidson Laura Simmons • Liz Seabrook • Maggie Li • Mark Leaver • Mitch Payne • Molly McArdle • Morgane Erpicum • Nathan Lunda Peter Marshall • Polina Vinogradova • Stephanie Draime

Design Your
Next Holiday

Visit our Travel Planner online to build a bespoke
guide based on insider recommendations

—

SEARCH
YOUR DESTINATION

*From effervescent capital cities
to bohemian beach towns*

SAVE
YOUR FAVOURITE PLACES

*Be it a local restaurant, off-grid
art gallery or subterranean bar*

SHARE
YOUR GUIDE

*Download, email to your friends
and share on social media*

SUITCASEMAG.COM/PLANNER

#SUITCASEtravels

We love sharing travel stories with our readers, but we want to hear about your adventures as well. Tag your Instagram photos #SUITCASEtravels to guide us around the globe – we'll regram our favourites and feature our top nine in each issue.

ananewyork
Havana, Cuba

ceri.harris
Mount Cook National Park, New Zealand

joethommas
Lisbon, Portugal

katherinemarycara
Bukhara, Uzbekistan

thetravelquandary
Lofoten Islands, Norway

nadia.ryan
Sintra, Portugal

acoffeeandapassport
Bran Castle, Romania

postcardsfromchristine
Zugspitze, Germany

wanderlost.and.found
Buffalo Beach, Western Australia

The
Pioneer
Issue

Words by
OLIVIA SQUIRE

My inbox is swamped with promises. My smartphone is full of snake-oil salesmen. And don't even get me started on the messiahs beaming from my television screen. It's a funny thing, our modern world of influence – of false prophets and pop idols, likes and heart-eyes. Against a backdrop of endless awards shows, hot lists and polarised politics, it can seem like we're drowning in visionaries. The notion of the pioneer has been aggressively packaged, marketed and sold, our hunger for something (or someone) to staple our hopes to diluting this very dream of a saviour just as the challenges facing us escalate.

However, every action breeds a reaction. As the cult of personality has resurfaced, so has the power of the movement. For our 25th issue we wanted to map the people and concepts daring to alter the way we travel – but rather than targeting "influencers" or tech billionaires, we discovered individuals and whole communities quietly carving out conduits for change and pioneering a new kind of world, for the planet and all those who inhabit it.

When it comes to safeguarding our environment, the African savannah has become a battleground in recent decades as its rarest species dwindle at the weapons of poachers. The travel company andBeyond is tackling the situation head-on with its innovative rhino translocation programmes in South Africa's KwaZulu-Natal province (p. 108). The champion freediver Hanli Prinsloo has spent much of her adult life below sea level – she recalls how her encounters with dolphins and whales triggered an all-consuming desire to preserve the sense of freedom she found there (p. 126).

Understanding the commonalities between ourselves and seemingly faraway places and people is essential in order to travel responsibly. I followed in the footsteps of earlier explorers to the vast, Arctic wilderness of Svalbard, where I discovered a community of souls determined to protect rather than plunder its threatened shores (p. 140). The photographer Chris Burkard has dedicated his work to exploring such remote lands – as he explains, "How can we expect change to occur in any capacity unless we show people why they should care?" (p. 156)

To pioneer often means to challenge our expectations. Indonesia's Banda Islands were once seen as a trading floor for precious nutmeg, but our writer established an altogether more peaceful synergy with its rolling waves and mountains (p. 116). In Madagascar our Digital Editor-in-Chief learned to abandon conventional travel narratives in an off-road expedition through its coastal villages (p. 88), while the photographer Aron Klein had to submit to the rigours of the winter reindeer migration alongside Norway's indigenous Sami tribe (p. 134).

Steve McCurry has forged a career from locating our shared humanity in his arresting portraits, often captured in times of conflict and strife (p. 80). Cities around the world are wrestling with shifting identities – in the Lebanese capital of Beirut contemporary creativity is attempting to heal a war-torn past (p. 72), whereas in the "swamp" of Washington DC art, activism and commerce are blending to question what it means to be an American today (p. 56).

In order to overcome external barriers we first need to unlock our own potential. A series of retreats in Italy (p. 36), Spain (p. 40) and Bali (p. 48) aim to equip guests with the tools to tackle obstacles, while on the other end of the spectrum "survivacations" use extreme experiences to spark internal transformation (p. 52). As the controlled use of psychedelics becomes more accepted, it's even possible that the next great journeys will take place within the parameters of our own minds (p. 44).

Above all, to be a pioneer today is to create space for change to occur. Twenty-five issues since we began, we feel hugely privileged to provide a platform for the destinations, concepts and communities that are mapping new routes across the globe.

SUITCASE
MAGAZINE

For the Pioneers

—

*Give someone a year's worth of travel
inspiration with a gift subscription*

1 Year | 4 Volumes | £30

The Wheel Thing

Crash Baggage
ICON Hard Cabin Trolley

L70cm x H45cm x W24.5cm
2.9kg
£195

Charting new waters often means picking up a few bumps and scratches along the way – something that Crash Baggage understands only too well. Its metallic cases arrive dented, Coke-can crumpled and in their words, "crashed", so that travellers can concentrate on the thrill of the journey ahead rather than worrying about keeping their suitcases pristine. The new ICON collection reinvents its trademark design with an enlarged size and even more resistant exterior. Yet it retains the "handle without care" philosophy that the brand's founder, Francesco Pavia, insists allows owners "freedom of movement and action wherever and whenever". The only remaining challenge is to get out there and add some texture of your own.

BOOKS & TRACKS

An Unnecessary Woman
RABIH ALAMEDDINE

NATHANIEL'S NUTMEG
GILES MILTON

THE AYE-AYE AND I   Gerald Durrell

THE BOY WHO HARNESSED THE WIND   WILLIAM KAMKWAMBA

NORTHERN LIGHTS
Philip Pullman

Heartburn   NORA EPHRON

ILLUSTRATION BY LAURA SIMMONS

Books

FOR THE BANDA ISLANDS
NATHANIEL'S NUTMEG
by Giles Milton

This history-slash-adventure book charts the 17th-century battle between the Dutch and English for the island of Run, which the nutmeg harvest turned into the most lucrative (and desirable) of the Banda Islands. Milton unravels a swashbuckling tale of colonial exploration and exploitation in the high seas.

FOR BEIRUT
AN UNNECESSARY WOMAN
by Rabih Alameddine

From her apartment in Beirut 72-year-old Aaliya secretly translates novels into Arabic, invoking a cast of literary characters from Dickens to Dostoyevsky. As a single woman in a culture where feminism has yet to take flight, literature becomes a kind of religion in this curious, complicated novel.

FOR MADAGASCAR
THE AYE-AYE AND I
by Gerald Durrell

Durrell, one of Britain's best-loved conservationists, brings his irreverent and eccentric approach to his final adventure in search of the Madagascan aye-aye, a type of lemur thought to be an omen of death. In its pursuit he encounters a host of other strange creatures alongside an equally unfamiliar way of life.

FOR MALAWI
THE BOY WHO HARNESSED THE WIND
by William Kamkwamba

When Kamkwamba was 14 years old he was forced to abandon his education to help his family tend to their crops amid a climate of drought and famine. This is the true story of his dream to build a windmill to supply electricity and running water to his village, as well as an example of how invention can overcome adversity.

FOR SVALBARD
NORTHERN LIGHTS
by Philip Pullman

The first book in Pullman's iconic His Dark Materials trilogy sees the heroine Lyra journey to Svalbard in search of her missing friend Roger and uncle Lord Asriel. Among the bleak white landscape and under the Northern Lights, she becomes embroiled in a treacherous quest aided by witches and the armoured bear Iorek Byrnison.

FOR WASHINGTON DC
HEARTBURN
by Nora Ephron

Ephron's whip-smart observations are applied to her own life in this thinly veiled semi-autobiographical novel about the breakdown of a marriage between food writer Rachel Samstat and political journalist Mark Feldman in Washington DC. Along the way she meshes laugh-out-loud one-liners with recipes for mashed potato and lima beans with pears.

Tracks

FOR THE BANDA ISLANDS
BAD NEWS
by Rollie

Hard psychedelia and funk might not be what comes to mind when you think of Indonesia, but Rollie's Hendrix vibes reveal another side to the country.

FOR BEIRUT
ABU ALI
by Ziad Rahbani

Beirut's current arts renaissance pays homage to the golden years of the 1970s, represented in this 1978 tune from Lebanese legend Rahbani.

FOR MADAGASCAR
MALOYA TON TISANE
by Michou

Hailing from nearby Réunion Island, the tropical rhythms of Michou are an infectious companion with which to explore off the beaten track.

FOR MALAWI
SKY ABOVE
by Malawi Mouse Boys

Scouted selling mice kebabs and with instruments made of scrap metal, this band's album was the first to be released in the Chichewa language outside Malawi.

FOR SVALBARD
HOLY LAND
by Jenny Hval

Norway's answer to Kate Bush, Hval's vast soundscapes and icy production will see you through the Arctic Circle's wildest fjords and mountains.

FOR WASHINGTON DC
THE SOUTH WILL NEVER RISE AGAIN
by Des Demonas

Garage rock meets psychedelia in this disorderly slice of state-of-the-nation music from the Washington DC natives Des Demonas.

100ml

1. Diego Dalla Palma Naked Symphony Multicolour Compact Powder Blush £27.50, **2. REN** Evercalm Overnight Recovery Balm £40, **3. Dr. Barbara Sturm** Facial Scrub £45, **4. Chanel** Le Volume Révolution Mascara £28, **5. NYDG** Re-Contour Eye Gel £17, **6. Aurelia Probiotic Skincare** Cell Repair Night Oil £62, **7. By Terry** Cellularose Brightening CC Serum £61, **8. Fresh** Limited Edition Zodiac Sugar Lip Treatment Advanced Therapy Pisces £21.50, **9. Jurlique** Sweet Peony & Tangerine Hydrating Mist Limited Edition £24, **10. Zoeva** Premiere Edition Luxe Classic Shader

11. Charlotte Tilbury Stars-In-Your-Eyes Palette *£60*, **12. Algenist** Genius Ultimate Anti-Aging Vitamin C+ Serum *£85*, **13. Sisley** Nutritive Lip Balm *£49.50*, **14. RéVive** Intensité Complete Anti-Aging Eye Serum *£220*, **15. Axiology** Natural Organic Lipstick in Joy *£24*, **16. Diptyque** Protective Moisturising Facial Lotion *£44*, **17. Dr Dennis Gross** Alpha Beta Exfoliating Moisturiser *£82*, **18. Susanne Kaufmann** St. John's Wort Bath *£39*, **19. Lixirskin** Soft Clay Rubber No-Bits Exfoliant and Mask In One *£28*, **20. Sarah Chapman** Skinesis Morning Facial *£49*.

The Pioneer Beauty Edit

Alex Box is a make-up artist and the former creative director of Illamasqua. She has created iconic looks for designers including Karl Lagerfeld, Alexander McQueen, Gareth Pugh and Vivienne Westwood, and is renowned for her experimental and often surreal looks, which chart the correlation between art, science, nature and the magical.

I have always seen beauty as an evolving paradigm. As a word it may fall in and out of favour, but it forever remains reflective of the times. I view myself as an artist looking in on the industry, exploring and challenging constructs of beauty to pioneer new ways of seeing. Intelligence, integrity and spirituality are the most under-used words in beauty, so that's what I strive to bring. My manifesto is to generate creative freedom, push boundaries and inspire others to do the same.

My style has evolved through fearlessness and being open to the moment, the cosmos and the muse. I've always talked about beauty being a journey of the soul and a spiritual swim in the understanding of one's uniqueness. The individual is the future – we hold everything we need to empower ourselves. We don't need to be told what is beautiful. I'm currently building a retreat to explore this concept of mindfulness within beauty.

My edit may not be what you'd expect, as I do not view beauty (or anything else) in a conventional way. My ritual more often involves chanting a yoga mantra or bathing in the feminine energy and healing power of the moon than indulging in the latest trend. These products allow me to keep challenging the status quo.

FUSHI
Triphala Capsules and Turmeric C3 & Bioperine Extract, *£8 and £20*
I couldn't choose between these two powerhouses of wellbeing. I was an early adopter of Ayurvedic remedies in the Nineties so have been taking them for a long time. The balance of the doshas has helped me to understand both minor and serious ailments.

SHU UEMURA
High Performance Balancing Cleansing Oil Advanced Formula, *£52*
This much-copied, never-beaten maverick product has been on my shelf for over 20 years. When I first left art college I worked for Shu Uemura. He was humble and full of excitement about the possibility of make-up. His vision was extraordinary.

VIJAYSHREE
Golden Nag Champa Incense Sticks, *£7.30*
I have many different types of incense varying in rarity and purpose, but this beautiful incantation of scent and spirit is the one I always return to. It's so full and nourishing.

THE MINERAL WAREHOUSE
Rose Quartz, *£17*
I've always carried crystals and have several for different purposes, but rose quartz is the mother. Calm, caring and clearing, it's the stone of love and protection.

LE LABO
Tonka 25 100ml, *£180*
I absolutely love Le Labo's fragrances, aesthetic and ethos. Every time I go into one of their boutiques they have a new and surprising twist on an old classic.

ORVEDA
Visibly Brightening & Skin Perfecting Masque, *£250*
This range was recommended to me by the beauty expert Edwina Ings-Chambers. She knows I'm a little obsessed with skincare and this product blew my mind. When something works this well, it feels like a requiem.

ILLAMASQUA
Gel Sculpt, *£25*
I left a proud legacy of Illamasqua products during my time there, of which this cult classic is one. It's the result of a brainwave I had to create a transparent contouring gel with a tint that would mimic the natural flush of a cheek.

Serena Guen

A journey to Thailand's remote city of **Chiang Rai** reminds
SUITCASE's founder and CEO of her inspiration
for starting the magazine

———

It was a frustration with existing travel narratives that drove me to create SUITCASE back in 2012, after I realised that there was a hunger to discover destinations outside of the average guidebook recommendations. Visiting Thailand's "Golden Triangle" city of Chiang Rai – so-called because of its location on the border of Thailand, Myanmar and Laos – reminds me of the importance of looking outside established tourist trails. Where other parts of Thailand remain dogged by huge tour groups, the remoteness of Chiang Rai means it retains a certain tranquillity and authenticity that I have often found lacking when travelling in this part of the globe.

My hotel, the Four Seasons Tented Camp Golden Triangle, is not your average luxury resort, something that dawns on me as soon as I arrive and am driven to my open-air spa room (one of only nine) in a 20-year-old, beaten-up Land Rover that needs to be jump-started en route. I'm later joined by a poisonous frog whose urine can supposedly blind you. The next day I wake up to the sounds of the Thai symphonic orchestra – elephants, cicadas and birds – as I look out over the thick and untamed jungle beyond, feeling as if I've escaped to another place and era.

I spend the majority of my time in Chiang Rai befriending an elephant named Luke Odd (which transforms from the pedestrian into the exotic when translated to "diamond" in Thai).

She's part of a local sanctuary that rescues elephants from the street and manual labour in various Asian countries. There are only 25 female elephants in the sanctuary at any one time and each is paired with a mahout (elephant trainer) and his family. Elephants are magnificent animals – they can remember up to 90 words and recognise a person after meeting them three times. It's magical to bathe, feed and walk Luke Odd, and I feel like I've built a special kind of companionship.

One day I cross the Thai border to a tiny village in Myanmar, where I discover the traditional delicacy of underground wasp larvae and watch the local women make a natural sun cream from tanaka wood. Returning to Thailand, however, the complexities of life for many living along the border are brought home to me when I visit the Karen people, who were once persecuted in Myanmar and continue to face similar issues in Thailand.

I meet a little girl in a princess dress wearing one of the thick, gold necklaces traditionally worn by the Karen women. They are extremely skilled craftspeople whom you can support by buying ethically sourced artefacts at Ways of Change, a co-creation brand connecting designers and refugee artisans to create change in the fashion industry. The initiative is a reminder that wherever we travel, we have a choice about how we interact with a destination – a belief that SUITCASE will continue to share.

FOUR SEASONS TENTED CAMP GOLDEN TRIANGLE · PHOTO BY KEN SEET

What a Place to be Alone

For the inaugural SUITCASE Magazine + Horizn Travel Club,
blogger and author Chidera Eggerue (also known as The Slumflower)
explores **Copenhagen**'s creative core with her bordeaux-hued
Horizn Model M in tow

Photos by **POLINA VINOGRADOVA**

I wrote my book What a Time to be Alone during a period in my life when nothing felt more appealing than finding solitude. Now I truly believe that it's the secret to unlocking your truest, deepest self – and that travelling solo is one of the most exciting ways to ease into your own company, especially when exploring somewhere as inclusive as Copenhagen.

If you're looking for a city where minding your business is the norm, this is the place for you. The locals have an effortless way of being welcoming without making you feel like you're being watched – touching down with my massive afro and flamboyant style, I notice a few people glance at me with a combination of curiosity and fascination, but never in an invasive way. This is very important to mention, especially for any black women who are considering visiting – there's a warmth to this city that immediately makes me feel at home.

Cosiness, I soon discover, is ubiquitous to Copenhagen. I begin with a hygge-inducing oat-milk latte at Prolog Coffee Bar, which arrives on a pastel-pink tray that I can't resist snapping pictures of. I head across the street and have the best burger of my life at the awesome Tommi's Burger Joint, which also makes incredible milkshakes. My home here is the gorgeous and very central Hotel Sanders, where I'm excited by the vintage-style bathroom but even more in love with the breakfast. Blueberry waffles? Yes please!

As someone who can't ride a bike despite being fully grown, being in Copenhagen makes me want to learn. The city's manageable size and structure mean that it's actually easier and quicker to cycle than it is to drive and I'm told that all the best parts of Copenhagen can be reached within ten to 20 minutes of pedalling. Renting a bike for the day is super cheap and, in some places, even free, although it's on foot that I set out to two of the key neighbourhoods on my list, Vesterbro and Nørrebro. If Vesterbro is the Brooklyn of Copenhagen, then Nørrebro is the Kreuzberg. Both are only a short walk from the city centre and are generous in their diversity, colour and spirit.

As a fashion lover the shop that captures my heart is the Danish brand Mads Norgaard, which specialises in streetwear with a slightly edgy twist. Before I leave I make sure to buy a leopard-print, utility-style jumpsuit, a striped satchel and a cosy hoodie dress to stuff into my Horizn Model M suitcase as a reminder of my time in this stylish Scandi capital. ▶▶

TOMMI'S BURGER JOINT

THE LOWDOWN

A travel brand paving its way alongside a global creative community, Horizn Studios is open, curious and dedicated to developing innovative products to make travel fun, easy and seamless. The SUITCASE Magazine + Horizn Travel Club builds on Horizn's international appeal by exploring the cities of the world through the eyes of some of our favourite creative influencers.

Horizn Model M Cabin Luggage 33L in Marsala
L55cm x H40cm x W20cm
3.4kg (hand luggage approved)
£329

Aerospace-grade polycarbonate hard shell	Inbuilt compression pad	One-year free access to Horizn GO travel service
Laundry bag	Four high-end Japanese 360° wheels (by Hinomoto)	Removable power bank
	Water-resistant front pocket	

STAY

HOTEL SANDERS

TORDENSKJOLDSGADE 15, 1055

hotelsanders.com

Rooms from £232

Supremely elegant and traditional yet also contemporary, Hotel Sanders aims to make your stay a curated experience – from suggesting popular food spots and lively local haunts to pointing you in the right direction for private boat hire. Founded by acclaimed former Royal Danish Ballet dancer Alexander Kølpin, the hotel uncoincidentally neighbours the Royal Danish Theatre. More taupe than theatrical, its bedrooms range from a cosy coupé to an indulgent apartment.

HOTEL SANDERS

EAT

LA BANCHINA

REFSHALEVEJ 141A, 1432

labanchina.dk

Located right on the water and secluded from the city, this 16-seat, farm-to-table restaurant is inspired by its natural surroundings, serving up organic vegetables and seafood.

LILLE BAKERY

REFSHALEVEJ 213A, 1432

lillebakery.com

Lille – meaning little – is a compact, open-kitchen bakery in the up-and-coming Refshaleøen district. Munch on something delicious from the tightly edited menu – the brioche with mascarpone and sour mirabelle plum is a standout.

TOMMI'S BURGER JOINT

WESTEND 13, 1661

burgerjoint.dk

A family establishment, Tommi's Burger Joint isn't the kind of place that does things on a small scale. From multiple toppings to XL fries and loaded burgers, go the whole hog and top it off with a strawberry milkshake.

LILLE BAKERY

SHOP

HAY HOUSE

ØSTERGADE 61, 1100

hay.dk/en-gb

A household name with an international reputation, Hay's second-floor shop on Østergrade is bright and spacious, showcasing a range of design pieces which are as beautiful as they are functional.

ATELIER SEPTEMBER

GOTHERSGADE 30, 1123

atelierseptember.dk

Appropriately located in the fashionable Gothersade neighbourhood, Atelier September epitomises design-forward Copenhagen. Its café/project room/creative studio hybrid has been a hallmark of Danish design since opening in 1987.

ACNE ARCHIVE

ELMEGADE 21, 2200

acnearchive.com

The Acne Archive, of which there are only three worldwide, sells classic styles and pieces from previous collections – selected pieces are marked down a hefty 75 per cent.

CIRKELBROEN

DO

CIRKELBROEN

APPLEBYS PLADS, 1411

Designed by Icelandic-Danish artist Olafur Eliasson, the Cirkelbroen (Circle Bridge) draws from the Christianshavn district's maritime history and culture. Visit in full light to see the five staggered circular platforms, each with their own "mast" which together form the silhouette of a sailing boat.

DESIGNMUSEUM DANMARK

BREDGADE 68, 1260

designmuseum.dk/en

Showcasing pieces created by renowned Danish names such as Arne Jacobsen and Poul Henningsen as well as designers from around the world, the museum's collections of fashion, ceramics, craft and furniture (expect to see a lot of chairs) are vast.

CENTRAL HOTEL & CAFÉ

TULLINSGADE 1, 1610

centralhotelogcafe.dk

This cosy café with a flair for vintage design is wedged between two cowering buildings and has a matchbox-sized hotel with just one bedroom perched atop it.

DRINK + DANCE

THE JANE

GRÅBRØDRETORV 8, 1154

thejane.dk

Hidden doors concealed by bookshelves reveal rooms within rooms in this labyrinthine cavern, where you can either snuggle up by the fire in an old Chesterfield or dance your way into the early hours of the morning.

ANDY'S BAR

GOTHERSGADE 33B, 1123

andysbar.dk

With its wooden benches, red walls, convivial lighting and warm pub atmosphere, Andy's Bar is an alluring spot for a casual evening tipple.

Home.Made

—

Tala Barbotin Khalidy

Tala Barbotin Khalidy's hand-embroidered, ready-to-wear collection
weaves together her Lebanese roots and NYC training while
challenging notions of fast fashion

Words by **CARLY SMITH**

The 21-year-old French-Lebanese designer Tala Barbotin Khalidy is part of a new vanguard of fashion pioneers working towards a future for the industry based on empathy, craft and concept. As a young girl growing up in Paris, Barbotin Khalidy fell in love with fashion and later moved to New York to study at Parsons, one of the city's most renowned schools for design. Here she became disheartened by the pace at which fast fashion forces designers to produce – but in recognising this frustration, she also found her niche.

Barbotin Khalidy's current collection is a rebellion against much that the industry represents. While fast fashion thrives on the dehumanisation of workers, her collection is a reflection of the emotions that make us human. She has also partnered with a New York-based women's advocacy initiative, Womankind, to host workshops centred on the therapeutic qualities of embroidery. At a local level the workshops provide much-needed relief and stimulate emotional and occupational growth for New York women who've experienced trauma, and on a more global level they challenge the fashion industry to help bring about social and cultural progress.

How has your dual nationality of French and Lebanese informed your approach to fashion?
Growing up in France there was always this idea of understated elegance, of not being too aggressive with clothes. However my family is also involved in the production of textiles in Lebanon and as a child I had access to an insanely developed culture around craftsmanship that encompassed fabrics, embellishments, colours, ample shapes and symbolic images. It's such a warm, extremely diverse culture, yet there is balance amid the craziness – for example wearing a traditional "abbaya" tunic with Converse shoes. That duality between French and Lebanese culture has definitely allowed me to cultivate a sense of balance and empathy.

Having a foot in both Western and Middle Eastern cultures means that I have experienced first-hand the blatant lack of knowledge towards other cultures in the West, which reached its peak when anti-immigration and racist rhetoric intensified in the United States in the wake of the 2016 election. Fast fashion definitely plays a part in this loss of curiosity because it promotes clothes that represent a quick solution and are void of meaning. If the clothes had intent, people would want to keep them, which would mean less financial gratification for the companies promoting fast fashion. I've decided to encourage culture, education and curiosity in my work as opposed to ignorance, hate and violence. It's why I'm revaluing Lebanese embroidery techniques, which are beginning to disappear, and reinterpreting them in contemporary ways when assembling and constructing my garments.

Can you explain your collaboration with Womankind?
I'm currently teaching embroidery as an occupational craft therapy at Womankind's residences in New York, targeting those who have experienced sexual or domestic violence and human trafficking. The workshops help participants to heal from trauma by developing their confidence, learning new skills and finding a nurturing platform to express themselves in ways that traditional therapy methods sometimes cannot accommodate. The idea was based on my research on how occupational craft therapy was used in the First World War to help bedridden soldiers in hospitals surpass trauma and emotionally heal.

What is the most rewarding part of the experience?
Seeing the participants' emotional progress and their growing curiosity. One woman became so excited about the workshops that she embroidered new pieces each week and sought me out for additional help. We spent a lot of time working together and she is now on her way to working in textiles herself. Another participant barely had any time to sew as she had to care for her

two young kids, so I would show her stitches and then watch her baby while she practised. Even though she was overwhelmed, she always came to the workshop and slowly built confidence in herself. When I presented the workshops at Parsons School of Design people came up to me afterwards to tell me about their personal experiences with abuse and how it affected their clothes, their bodies and their states of mind. It was so powerful that I get emotional just talking about it. My relationship to design is even more mindful of others now. The discussions that we had in the workshops influenced my designs to the core, resulting in a more collaborative design process.

How else do you hope to act differently from other companies within the fashion industry?
I would love to create a collaborative space where there is an exchange of information and skills from all cultures and ages that would help foster creative design solutions. There are already companies that are exploring more ethical pathways into design and associations that offer craft workshops, but there is rarely any correlation between the two. Creating a space where there is learning on both sides – people learning about design craft and culture, and designers learning about people's needs and experiences – is the kind of initiative that will begin to heal society and is the kind of space I want to take up.

What does it mean to you to be a young creative? What responsibilities do you feel are tied to this?
Someone once told me that my work was as if "concept and sustainability had a baby with craft". I don't think young creatives necessarily need to feel pressure to be socially engaged in their work, but I do feel like we have a responsibility to create alternatives that will draw people in and make them feel something, especially because we are increasingly learning to desensitise ourselves through phones, fast fashion, by abandoning culture and knowledge, or with walls of emotional defence.

How do you think fashion has the potential to take on new meanings in the future?
I am very hopeful for the future of fashion, as I see the diverse ways that young designers are tackling issues in the industry. The good news is that investors in companies across all industries are now asking about sustainability as a measure of future profit. They recognise the value it has and companies without a plan including sustainability efforts are less likely to be backed – it's a mark of the future. I genuinely believe that fashion has the potential to educate and to incite curiosity, culture, poetry and rebellion. At its core, fashion has always been a catalyst of movements and it is my hope that it will continue to play that role in the future.

Erg Chebbi

Sahara Desert, *Morocco*

Words and photos by
MORGANE ERPICUM

I find myself in front of Erg Chebbi, one among the oceans of dunes on the western edge of the Sahara Desert. Like a border scored in the sand, all infrastructure abruptly ends at Erfoud a few miles down the road. Civilisation gives way to the hamada's rocky textures and further on the horizon the Erg's sweeping, shimmery expanse.

Shelter, paramount amid the austerity of such a landscape, is impermanent and primitive – threadbare rugs underfoot, a tarp overhead and a firepit dug in the sand. When lost in the immensity of the desert, time seems to fluctuate. Fleeting, kaleidoscopic moments of intense, soul-wrenching beauty at sunrise and sunset rapidly succeed one another, sandwiched between languid hours of exhausting heat and frigid nights.

Tradition holds great importance to the Berber peoples inhabiting the Sahara. Techniques used for thousands of years have yet to be bettered by any modern equivalent. Earthy tagines slow-cooked on embers, daily afternoon siestas that provide respite from the scorching sun, nightly gatherings around the fire – all stem from a routine based first and foremost on the freedom to live in one of the most inhospitable places on earth.

Wake up Here

---

40 Winks

Stepney Green, *London*

Words by **INDIA DOWLEY**

"The attributes we look for in the perfect guest include: a lively sense of humour, good manners, a keen mind, irrepressible curiosity, a sociable disposition, childlike enthusiasm and a fondness for spirited banter. A love of art and design obviously helps too."

Thus the tone is set for the world's first "micro boutique hotel" – and rightly so, for with just two rooms and a salaciously glamorous history, encapsulated in the devilishly flamboyant proprietor, Mr David Carter, and his enviable selection of hats, 40 Winks can afford to be picky when it comes to who's sleeping over.

Crossing the threshold of this dimly lit townhouse in Mile End is akin to stepping into a seductive cabinet of curiosities which disorientate and delight from the moment you clasp the lion-head door knocker. For years the location of high-profile shoots and fashion editorials, gilt walls and a fuchsia-pink velvet staircase set the scene for a fantasia of whimsy created under Carter's wickedly sharp eye.

Jewels and feathers, silk poufs, antique dolls, Persian carpets, architectural mirrors, pom-pom chandeliers, vintage busts and countless trinkets all find a place in this avant-garde home-from-home – as will you, as guests are encouraged to treat it as their own (there's no mercantile handing over of a credit card on arrival here).

Monthly "bedtime story nights" see au fait urbanites don lustrous nightwear for an evening of intoxicating tipples and tales that feels like a secret club – you'll know you're part of it when David throws a "dahhling" in your direction. More than one guest has described the experience of staying here as "life-changing" – though perhaps their sojourn coincided with one of the séances...

Rooms from £120
40winks.org

CALDERA HOUSE

JACKSON HOLE, *WYOMING*

This just-opened hotel and members' club provides a refreshingly antler-free spin on the ski lodge concept, with a slick design that includes lots of covetable furniture and not a taxidermied moose in sight. Come snow or shine there's a host of luxurious experiences to choose from, whether hitting the slopes with an Olympic skier or biking with Lance Armstrong himself.

700,000 HEURES

ANGKOR, *CAMBODIA*

Billed as "the first wandering hotel in the world", 700,000 Heures is the dreamchild of theatrical entrepreneur Thierry Teyssier. Every six months the concept moves to a new location where Teyssier unfolds a host of unique, time-limited experiences – candlelit dinners in temples, a day at the circus and collecting water hyacinths by boat for its current Cambodian incarnation.

SHIPWRECK LODGE

SKELETON COAST, *NAMIBIA*

Known as "the land God made in anger", Namibia's Skeleton Coast is an eerie take on the safari experience. Thousands of shipwrecks scatter the coast and you're as likely to spot a whale as a giraffe. Inspired by the carcasses of boats and whales, the lodge remains a cosy spot to stare out at the surrounding solitude.

Eremito,

Umbria, *Italy*

Words and photos by
HOLLY TUPPEN

The combined assault of the thunder rumbling overhead and the Gregorian chants drifting from within makes crossing Eremito's threshold every bit as dramatic as I'd hoped. It's taken me one plane, several trains and an off-road jeep to arrive at this hotel deep in the Umbrian hills, drawn by the promise of 3,000 hectares of wilderness, time to myself, long moments of silence and a true digital detox – as well as the intriguing paradox of a "luxury monastic retreat". My pilgrimage to get here may have ended, but I sense that my journey has only just begun.

Despite having the appearance of an ancient monastery, Eremito is only five years old. The hotel took four years to build using 130,000 stones and relying entirely on ancient Italian masonry techniques combined with state-of-the-art solar and geothermal heating systems. Contemplating the extent of this commitment is part of the appeal – it's the antithesis of logic and the fruition of the owner's slightly mad vision.

Light years away from the monotonous luxury of other Instagram-ready hotels, Eremito is a pleasant assault on the senses containing pockets of a Moroccan riad, an Umbrian family home and a 14th-century Franciscan monastery. Repurposed glass, wood, brass and fabrics add slices of the unexpected to its otherwise minimal design. Its narrow, candle-lit corridors, textured walls and weathered stone floors can feel a little foreboding, yet the living room is as homely as can be and is filled with sprawling cushions, antique curiosities and sunflowers.

Eremito's lovable boxer dog, Pepo, leaps up to welcome me as I'm ushered to my celluzze, one of 12 rooms based on Franciscan monks' cells. We pass the plunge pool, reading cave, Giardini di Silencio (Silent Garden) and a small family chapel before reaching a perfectly formed room at the end of a long, quiet corridor. It feels luxurious in its simplicity – there's a wrought-iron bed with soft white linen, a marble sink with home-made soap and fresh, cool air seeps in from the forested valley below. Over the next 48 hours, waking up comes as readily as sleep. ▶▶

It's difficult to appreciate Eremito without first getting to know its owner, Marcello Murzilli. Marcello has a natural flair for storytelling and within moments of our meeting he begins emphatically: "In my life, I've always been more interested in the creative format than repeating the same things over and over. Eremito is a concept that should be taken all over the world, but I don't want to do that. I enjoy creating new things."

It's an ethos that has served him well. After founding the Italian fashion line El Charro at 40, he "bought his freedom", sailed the world on a wooden boat, fell in love with a nature reserve in Mexico and built the eco-lodge Hotelito Desconocido before returning to his home country in search of something new. "I wanted to create a type of hotel that no-one had ever seen before – somewhere for people to come on their own and where spirituality and ecology come first."

Marcello's words leave me dancing somewhere between scepticism and enlightenment. So much of the modern world feels inherently bad for our mental health yet being bombarded with messages about disconnecting is tiresome – is it just another marketing buzzword akin to wellness, luxury and sustainability?

Adamant that this is a hotel for "everyday" people, not monks or those in need of therapy, Marcello urges me to switch off my phone and simply enjoy the space. The more he talks, the more

I feel as though I'm in a counselling session. "Society is built to make you unhappy and anxious. The demands on you are too big. We all need a place where we can strip everything back." He talks about the importance of prioritising and balance, getting rid of friends we don't need and focusing on one thing at a time. Finally, he warns me of the "Eremito effect": "Some come for a week, they change and reset – and then return for six months."

A small bell rings for dinner and the quiet descends. Unlike so many other wellness retreats, there's no schedule at Eremito except for meal times. Breakfast and lunch are lively, but the communal dinner is hosted in complete silence. We file tentatively into the dining room where candles flicker, the windows are flung open and dusk billows in. Birdsong, Gregorian chants and a soft clinking from the kitchen are the only sounds to be heard. The initial strangeness soon washes over (aided by my first gulp of red wine) and I relish giving such a perfectly formed meal my undivided attention.

Giddiness-inducing digestivos are taken around the bonfire and a gentle whirr of chatter fills the night sky. A mix of women and men from all over Europe, mostly travelling alone and in their 30s, have come here for time out, time alone and to switch off. The conversation runs freely, noticeably uninterrupted by the impulse to check in on somewhere or someone else with a quick glance at a screen. I'm reminded of what makes travel so

compelling – removed from preconceptions or routine, people are more open and honest. Bonds with strangers are fleeting yet at the same time meaningful.

The next morning I wake as dawn breaks and a thick mist creeps over the valley. After a morning prayer in the tiny chapel in the eaves, where Marcello, his brother and other staff members sing Italian verses to Pepo's rhythmic snoring, it's time for yoga.

We follow Marcello's lead through simple stretches and gentle meditation as the morning sun seeps in. As a stiff-jointed atheist, it's an unprecedentedly flexible and holy start to the day. Breakfast is less worthy – piles of cake, bread, pecorino cheese, tomatoes, granola, fruit and yoghurt, all home-made or home-grown – are washed down with several cups of punchy Italian coffee. Marcello announces, "We've awakened the soul, we've awakened the body and now it's time for coffee".

Reading, chatting and walking fill the rest of my time. I stomp into the hills to the tiny hamlet of Cantone and what looks like a mass of green trees from my celluzze turn red, orange, purple and silver on closer inspection. Butterflies dance around my shoulders and grasshoppers bounce off my ankles. Elderly men and women look bemused to see me meandering past their open homes until, without warning, the road dissipates into an olive grove. I stumble back into an impromptu pasta-making lesson run by

Sergio, Marcello's brother and Eremito's chef. The conversation dips between Italian and English as several of us make penchi pasta shapes from fresh dough in the dappled sunlight.

Leaving is an unexpected wrench. With so few decisions to make, people to please and demands to meet, being at Eremito is akin to a big, unanticipated hug. Marcello's warning swirls around my head – disconnecting can make much of modern life seem futile and even arduous.

I remember the pasta-making, the bonfire and the hikes. What made those moments enduring wasn't anything to do with praying, being surrounded by wilderness or disconnecting at all – in fact, it was making the effort to truly connect with everything around me. I put my phone away for a little longer.

THE LOWDOWN

Rooms from £125
eremito.com

easyJet flies to Rome from London several times a day from £39 per person
easyjet.com

Skin Deep

A combination of modern Western medicine and holistic Eastern philosophies trigger an emotional transformation at **Altea**'s SHA Wellness Clinic

———

Words and photos by
ABIGAIL LOWE

As a child, my dream in life was simple. I wanted to change my name to Amanda, have two children by the age of 26 and be an audacious chain smoker. Disappointingly – despite setting the bar exceedingly low – I've not managed to achieve any of those things, so I've been forced to downgrade my ambitions. Now my moment of zenith will come when I fully morph into Marion Cotillard. This may seem ludicrously unattainable, but from what my child-bearing friends have told me, channelling French sass and dying my hair is going to be a lot easier than birthing two babies (I'm now 34) and taking up an extremely expensive habit that makes me wheeze (I'm asthmatic). Plus, I've become quite attached to my name.

It's funny though, because there's beauty to be found in the naivety of my seven-year-old self. The goals I set back then were constructed in a time before health, love and money worries, before life did its characteristically chaotic thing and swept me up in a confusing cascade. That's not to say that life until now has been terrible – far from it – but tiptoeing through each day, desperately trying not to stray from the tightrope while swerving heartache, headache and harm as they come hurtling towards you at 100mph, can take its toll. Negotiating life's peaks and troughs is exhausting – no wonder we lose enthusiasm and motivation and our health and self-worth suffers, and no wonder navigating a way back to the optimistic soul who just wanted to smoke cigarettes seems insurmountable.

The truth is, it's rare that the flame of innocence is completely snuffed out. A scintilla of sparkle always remains buried within us somewhere – it's just a case of digging it out. And that's where places like SHA Wellness Clinic in Spain's Altea region can help.

Unlike most other spas, SHA's primary focus is to educate, raise awareness and arm guests with the tools and knowledge required to instigate a renewed sense of purpose. They do this by fusing the technologies and developments of Western medicine with holistic Eastern philosophies – as well as by delving into every nook and cranny of your being, before boldly highlighting where your problems lie and what steps you should take if you're keen to change them. Then it's up to you to stride outside the boundaries of the space-age, five-star set-up and start applying it all. Sounds overwhelming? It is, a little. But luckily SHA equips you well – its award-stacked shelves are testament to the fact.

Regardless, I'll admit that I'm a little nervous before embarking on this particular trip. In recent years I've had a recurrence of a childhood skin condition that's battered me both physically and mentally. In the process of trying to overcome it I've tried a variety of weird and wonderful treatments – some mainstream, others more obscure – but nothing has worked. The crushing disappointment that comes when I bow to another defeat in the battle against my own body is tough, so in the face of all new suggestions, I'm sceptical. (Plus, it took the Buddha 49 days of

›

stillness to reach enlightenment – I've only got two days, three nights and a mind that wanders through Rihanna's back catalogue every time there's silence). Nevertheless, I remain hopeful that surrendering to the darkness will allow a little bit of light to creep in, and maybe, with all its high-tech, innovative treatments, SHA will finally provide some of the answers I'm seeking.

The drive to the clinic does its best to dampen my positivity. The sky is a melancholy shade of dusty, leaden black, lightning strikes pierce the horizon like a beaten-up voodoo doll and as we course past the towering, bizarrely gothic skyline of Benidorm, a cantankerous grumble echoes through the air – pathetic fallacy is doing a faultless job of communicating how I'm feeling.

However, within the hour I find myself lying on a squishy, king-size bed looking out onto the glittering lights of Altea below, with the result that my anxieties have mostly subsided. Tomorrow I'm set to embark on the clinic's Discovery programme and according to my schedule, I'll be pampered with no less than two massages, two body wraps and a facial in-between bouts of burrowing into my deepest, darkest secrets. If that doesn't make me sleep soundly, nothing will.

The following morning I head to breakfast on the clinic's spectacular rooftop terrace – infinity pool included – overlooking the mountains and the Mediterranean beyond. Two things become immediately clear. One: wearing a robe 24/7 is what we do now. Two: diet plays a pivotal role in the SHA ethos. The founder Alfredo Bataller cured his own chronic illness through a combination of diet and naturopathy, so every dish on each of the restaurant's three menus (a doctor prescribes the most appropriate depending on your physical condition) is highly alkalising, balanced and nutrient-rich, as well as utterly delicious. Over the next few days consultations with a nutritionist, a bespoke cooking lesson and gallons of miso soup reaffirm how important diet is for helping to treat skin issues from the inside out, and is one of the most poignant lessons I take home with me.

As the days unfold and I march from one appointment to the next my doubts begin to melt away. It's inspiring to be in the presence of so many qualified experts and empowering to receive simple advice that has the potential to be life-changing. A therapist recommends spending more time on creative pursuits to de-stress, a factor that directly impacts skin. "If you ignore your creativity you end up feeling like you're missing something,"

she explains. "And you look to replace it – often with damaging things." A personal trainer demonstrates that my shoulders lack mobility and advises exercises to improve the problem. A cognitive assessor points to a jagged red trench on a chart and notes that my kidneys aren't performing as well as they should be, a sentiment echoed by a traditional Chinese medicine practitioner when she measures my pulse. "You're lacking in vitality, so take note of how you eat and sleep," she says. "It's important to strengthen from within."

If I'm honest, a lot of this information I already knew but for whatever reason hadn't fully acknowledged. As a result I find these revelations intensely emotional. I sob while being plied like ciabatta dough on the massage table and internally at the spa circuit when a particularly ferocious water jet tears my bikini bottoms off. But with these realisations comes a sense of release and a newfound confidence that with time, bodies, minds and bruises from the past can heal, and when you tackle a problem from all angles, its chances of survival are slashed. I've always been fascinated by the symbiosis of the internal and external, and my time at SHA emphasises the importance of working on both elements in order to improve either.

The rehabilitation process continues on a yoga mat, where I flex both my hamstrings and my soul, and while walking at a much faster pace than I'd like up a mountain. Admittedly it's worth the effort once I see the sun peek over the ridgeline. During my final meal a sulky cloud with a luminescent silver lining appears in the sky and every guest throws down their forks and runs to take a picture, desperate to document this literal marker of optimism. Suddenly it strikes me: it's not definitive answers we're searching for here, but rather a small flame of hope. Perhaps the biggest fight we ever have to overcome is that with ourselves and often our most potent weapon is reassurance that change is possible, in whatever form that might be. For now I've waved goodbye to Amanda – and reluctantly, to Marion – and instead I'm learning, gently and tenderly, to be comfortable in my own skin.

THE LOWDOWN

The Discovery Programme starts from £1,110 (excluding accommodation). Rooms from £275 per night
shawellnessclinic.com

43

The Best Trip

As micro-dosing, canna-tourism and virtual reality become more mainstream, are the new frontiers of transformative travel actually located within?

Words by **JAMES DAVIDSON**
Illustrations by **MAGGIE LI**

Robert Gordon Wasson was an atypical psychonaut – an inquisitive Wall Street banker drawn to Mexico by an interest in wild mushrooms. In a small Mazatec village in the mountains of Oaxaca he would meet María Sabina, a farmer and part-time spiritual healer who would be regarded as one of her country's great poets, yet die as poor as she was born. The banker's fortunes were destined to be different. Having bent the truth to secure his time with Sabina and her "magic" mushrooms, his transformative experience would be written up in Seeking the Magic Mushroom, a now infamous Life magazine article from 1957. Things would never quite be the same again.

By the mid-1900s natural hallucinogens had drifted into plain view via articles such as Wasson's and free-form literature from the Beat Generation. The 1960s took the spirituality of self-transcendence and daubed it in brilliant kaleidoscopic visuals, dancing it through fields and putting a flower in its hair. "He crashed around America selling 'consciousness expansion' without ever giving a thought to the grim meat-hook realities that were lying in wait for all the people who took him seriously," scrawled Hunter S. Thompson of Timothy "turn on, tune in, drop out" Leary in his gonzo masterpiece Fear and Loathing in Las Vegas.

But dust settles and the pendulum of psychedelia is swinging back to its roots in science and mental health. At a 2006 symposium celebrating his 100th birthday, Francis Crick – the Nobel Prize-winning father of modern genetics – revealed that he was under the influence of the "wonder child" lysergic acid diethylamide when he discovered the double-helix structure of DNA. Silicon Valley is also turning its attention to the body and mind, with the trends for fasting and micro-dosing leading the charge. Without the backdrop of the San Francisco scene's swirling concert posters or the soundtrack of George Harrison plucking a sitar, psychedelics are gaining a more credible reputation. Will the next stage of transformative travel be played out within us? ►►

Much has been made of the surge of interest in ayahuasca, an ancient Amazonian hallucinogenic brew typically administered by shamans under ceremonial conditions. Billed by The New Yorker as "the drug of choice for the age of kale", the potent psychedelic has found itself an uneasy poster child for a renewed interest in "psychospirituality", with millennials flocking to South America in a bid to expand their cosmic consciousness. It's easy to dismiss the Brooklynification of anything, but as quarter-of-a-billion-dollar apps like Headspace and Calm have taken meditation to the masses, ayahuasca's ability to reconnect the mind and soul to nature means that interest in it is unlikely to reverse, especially while it remains legal in certain countries.

The problem? As is often the case with the clumsy-footed West, spiralling prices for a scarce resource is taking it out of the hands of the Amazonian tribes who have used it as medicine for thousands of years. One luxury retreat offering "gourmet ayahuasca-appropriate meals" and one-on-one ceremonies with shamans advertises prices starting from £7,850 per guest. Another has positioned itself for entrepreneurs, offering programmes for "business leaders, start-up founders and thought leaders". For a generation fixated on issues like plastic straws, many still charge through life oblivious to sustainability issues until they become a digestible trend. Sure, there is value to be had in undertaking rituals largely unchanged to those Wasson experienced in the mid-20th century – but should the mindfulness minutes you've built up on your smartphone have taught you anything, it's to move with heedfulness and respect.

Inspired by a new wave of clinical trials using hallucinogens to assist in relieving anxiety and existential distress in terminally ill cancer patients, American author and journalist Michael Pollan's foray into transcendentalism – documented in his brilliant book How to Change Your Mind – is a far cry from the consciousness-contorting hedonism of the 1960s. Moreover, his research delineates a potential near-future for psychoactive substances where their interaction with wellness is more profound than a Beat Generation-inspired pilgrimage to Peru. Far from an argument for the recreational use of psychedelic drugs, Pollan's musings ponder the legitimate existence of mental health spas, where experts offer a guided psychedelic experience using nothing but our bodies and the depths of our consciousness as stimulation.

Stanislav Grof, an early advocate of LSD, developed a breathing technique he called Holotropic Breathwork upon the drug's prohibition in 1966. Said to induce an altered state of consciousness, alternate pairs of "breathers" and "sitters" ensure that it is a guided and safe experience. Grof calls it an "expanded cartography of the human psyche" and many of those who've undertaken his programmes claim to have relived their own birth simply from combining conscious control with breathing. While something that lies at the more outré corners of a movement that incorporates more accessible practices, breathwork, as countless articles will contest, is seen as one of the next big things in wellness.

As the millions of newcomers to meditation will have noted, breathing is an integral part of accessing our intuition. It's where our consciousness and subconscious meet and where we can begin to exert control over the parts of ourselves that are usually exerting control over us. As mindfulness has overtaken Ayurveda as the buzzword on spa menus across the world, expect breathwork to accompany yoga and meditation in the wellness revolution. Be it mental health spas where veritable psychedelic experiences aid issues such as depression or addiction or lite updates on Grof's path to out-of-body experiences, consciousness expansion is the new currency in wellness.

As the sniggering that surrounds New Age's perceived corniness has been dampened by a mainstream adoption of meditative practices, today's great explorers are becoming those who are journeying within. We are plotting new maps of the mind – and these paths might help us reroute millennials from Amazon's rainforests. The future of psycho-travel might look like MycoMeditations – an outfit hosting seven- and ten-day psilocybin-assisted therapy escapes in Jamaica – or Ganja Goddess Getaway, a cannabis-fuelled women's retreat that lives by the principles of "self-love, inclusivity, empathy, good fun and mindfulness". It could definitely look like the buoyancy that cannabis tourism is enjoying following America's dramatic perception shift when it comes to marijuana. It might simply be a case of virtual reality. Whatever it is, we need to understand that the future of travel could be separated from the physical notion of transport – that "travel" is a matter of perception. Our grasp of what goes on inside our minds is as deficient as our understanding of the deepest waters or farthest reaches of the galaxy. The new frontiers lie within.

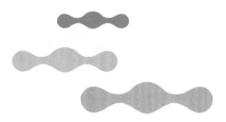

Powerful Possibility

Cliff jumping and unlocking potential in the paradise of **Bali**

———

Words by **DERVLA LOULI**
Photos by **CRILLE RASK**

PHOTO BY THEO WIDHARTO

It's 5am, my alarm clock is ringing and someone is knocking on my villa door. It's time for my first full day at Chōsen Experiences. My fellow participants join me for coffee, chia pudding and a breakfast smoothie. The bright-orange sunrise is painting palm-tree reflections in the pool and we all admire the quintessential postcard view of paradise. I drink a glass of cold brew as I read over my itinerary for the day. Two words – "cliff jumping" – stand out a little bolder than the rest and I can't tell if the swell of anxiety in the pit of my stomach is from the extra-strong coffee or because I'm terrified of heights.

I am here for a week-long journey that promises to challenge me physically and mentally while helping me to unlock my full potential. Founded by Robin Connelly and John Stanton, each Chōsen Experience includes adventure, fitness, nutrient-dense food, workshops, experiential learning, mindfulness and much more. Participants complete in-depth lifestyle questionnaires at the point of booking before groups of no more than ten meet at luxury properties in breathtaking locations in Bali (where I am now), Iceland, Guatemala, New Zealand and Cape Town.

Four-poster beds, infinity pools and manicured gardens are the norm for the properties in each region, and there's little to no single-use plastic used on site. The programming is designed by leading nutritionists, Olympic athletes and doctors, who ensure guests are perfectly fuelled, rested and challenged. It's essentially an "ideal week" where all the basics are taken care of so you can focus on the physical and mental challenges presented to you.

Like most of the group I learned about the experiences from a friend who is a member of the Chōsen Alumni community, a network of former participants who live in major cities around the world. The Alumni come from all walks of life but have one thing in common: a willingness and desire to continuously improve themselves mentally, physically, professionally and personally. My friend has joined me for the week and in addition to the two of us, the group is made up of a luxury fashion retail director, acclaimed writer and TV presenter, impact investor, freshly graduated tech major, successful bakery-chain entrepreneur, the founders John and Robin, and Chōsen's phenomenal chef, Josh Davies. We have flown in from all corners of the world and are ready for a transformational week.

We make our way in a convoy of cars to some waterfalls for our cliff-jumping and canyoning adventure. A chilled playlist begins, conversation flows and connections are made as John and Robin answer all our questions about the week. Before I know it we're in the water, rappelling down waterfalls and sliding over the river.

My cunning plan of keeping my fear of heights a secret is foiled when an extremely high cliff jump emerges. I go pale, pretend I'm being polite by letting everyone go ahead of me and try to delay the inevitable. I then turn to Josh with a million excuses on the tip of my tongue, who, without a second of hesitation, proceeds to give me a "leap of faith" pep talk. It works: I jump. The crowd cheers. So far, so good. Within minutes of hitting the water I'm climbing back up to the highest point and making myself jump over and over again. On my final jump something shifts and the fear that had been holding me back since I was a child is gone. It's the first breakthrough of many during the week. In less than 24 hours two of us have overcome a formerly debilitating fear of heights. I'm impressed.

Back at the luxurious villa we gather around the table for one of many delicious, healthy meals. Breakfast, lunch and dinner are family-style, wholefood feasts and everyone is encouraged to sit next to new people at every meal. This is not a weight-loss retreat, but guests often look and feel leaner when leaving thanks to the organic, unprocessed food. I have some of the best meals of my life during the week and everyone is impressed at how well their food intolerances, allergies and preferences are catered for. My digestive system has never been happier.

Every day of the week is programmed very carefully and includes different physical and mental activities. The only permanent daily items on the agenda are meal times and sunset yoga every evening before dinner. The instructors are phenomenal and this week include Olympic-gold swimmer Ryk Neethling, yoga and life coach Rachel Fearnley, clinical nutritionist Elisa Haggarty and the best local athletes in Bali. We are pushed to our limits during group workouts and gently nudged to the edge of our comfort zone, encouraged to open up and put in the work. The breakthroughs continue as someone learns how to swim, overcoming a childhood fear of open water.

John and Robin are former clean-tech venture capitalists who originally created Chōsen Experiences to balance their stressful work lives. Their original concept continues to develop and improve, and new aspects are regularly incorporated. This idea of continuous learning is one of my biggest takeaways from the week. Experts take part in activities and workshops alongside us and we have endless opportunities to learn from them. I decide to give up processed food and sugar for 30 days after a chat with Elisa, my freestyle becomes more efficient after a one-on-one, ten-minute lesson with Ryk, and I learn about the power of breath from Rachel. I feel like a child again, absorbing new experiences like a sponge. ▶▶

I should be exhausted from the workouts, adventures and workshops, but instead I have more energy than I've had in years. Downtime is taken seriously and there are dedicated chill-out times scattered throughout the week. Massages, physiotherapy and chiropractor sessions are all part of the process and the daily yin yoga is purposefully designed to lower cortisol levels. Bedtimes are early and eight hours of sleep are encouraged. We rise with the sun and start winding down at sunset so that by the time we've finished our post-dinner herbal tea the only thing we're craving is a night in our mosquito net-enveloped bed.

My second breakthrough happens during a goal-setting workshop led by John. We're asked to write down some goals, then choose one and break it down into bite-sized, actionable steps that we can take over the next three, six and nine months. My goal is career-orientated and entails quitting my current job, getting a position in the best lifestyle publishing house in my region and setting up my own business.

It seems impossible when I first write it down, but gradually over the hour the impossible begins to seem less so. There's something about writing it down and saying it out loud that makes it much more tangible and less of a dream. I discover I'm brave enough

to resign from my job, experienced enough to get the job I desire and determined enough to launch my own wellness retreat booking portal, Compare Retreats. In short, I begin to believe in myself and replace self-doubt with a sense of curiosity.

This combination of physical, mental and spiritual rituals is nothing short of extraordinary. We're all full of energy and raring to get to work on our individual goals. On our last night we gather around a fire on the beach at sunset and burn pieces of paper inscribed with things that we want to let go of. It's cathartic and we all enjoy a moment of collective silence staring into the fire, knowing we can accomplish any challenge we choose.

THE LOWDOWN

Chōsen Experiences' week-long retreats occur in multiple destinations throughout the year. Rooms for the Bali retreat from £4,145 per person per week (sharing) or £5,295 per person per week (single)

chōsenexperiences.com

Reborn Survivors

A new wave of adventures into the extreme unknown are seeing travellers journey into their deepest selves

Words by **RAE BOOCOCK**

From your seat in the helicopter, the Pearl Islands of Panama appear as if painted on a postcard. Rich jungle interiors framed by flaxen sand give way to cerulean water. This is Eden, you think... until the engine falters. Forced to make an emergency jump into the sea, you scramble ashore, visions of utopia floating away with the surf. You're stranded, Robinson Crusoe-style. Rescue is days away. Until then any hope of food, water or shelter rests on your sun-beaten shoulders.

Sound like your ideal getaway? Didn't think so. Yet this experience, offered by extreme adventure agency Bushmasters, is symptomatic of a shift in the way we think about travel. Gone are cut trails, luxury lodges and high-speed internet. In this Desert Island course you're taught the basics needed to survive before going it alone. You must make seawater drinkable, source food, start a fire, improvise shelter and make use of wreckage from the feigned helicopter crash. You'll deal with the psychological effects of isolation too – and bugs. Lots of them.

Former British Army officer Ian Craddock founded Bushmasters to fill a void for those yearning for an exciting, extreme and remote experience. "Be warned: it is not intended for people who want to waltz into the jungle or desert," he says. "Our trips are designed for those willing to push themselves."

Of course, travel that tests our physical and mental limits is no new phenomenon. Explorers have long braved inhospitable landscapes to chart new territory. Ultra-marathons are getting ever more extreme – on one seven-day, non-stop, 400km race across the Gobi Desert runners face wild dogs, a 3,000m mountain and temperatures spanning -20°C to 30°C. Astronauts signed up to the 2024 Mars One mission have no return ticket.

The difference is that it's now more than just the lionhearted few willing to venture beyond their comfort zone. Our love of survival stories – from Homer's Odyssey to The Hunger Games and Bear Grylls' The Island – is being translated into reality by travel companies with real-life adventurers at the helm. Those with enough mettle – and money – can brand cattle with vaqueros in the Guyanese savannahs, join West Bank locals for knafeh, trek with nomads across the Sudanese desert or snow kite across the Antarctic ice plains.

"Survivacations" are in vogue. But why? Are we not under enough pressure in our daily lives? How can we fight the flames of burnout by increasing our vulnerability? The answer is twofold. Firstly, the motivations behind adventure travel are shifting. A 2005 survey by the Adventure Trade Travel Association found that notions of "risk" and "danger" appealed to adventure travellers.

> 66 Our love of survival stories is being translated into reality by travel companies with real-life adventurers at the helm"

Yet when their pulse was taken again in 2017, it was the concepts of transformation, learning and expanded horizons that got hearts beating. Personal fulfilment is the new aspiration. As travel becomes a conduit for self-actualisation, so the goal of extreme adventure is shifting towards enriching the internal lives of travellers as they explore outwardly.

"Life is to be experienced," says Alvaro Cerezo, the founder of Docastaway, which strands clients on some of the world's last uncharted islands. His escapades are less about survival than unadulterated seclusion, hence why they vary in levels of intensity. In Comfort Mode guests stay in luxury lodgings and eco-resorts across the Philippines and Indonesia, and even in Survival Mode, more akin to a true castaway experience, additional provisions are on offer, be they modern camping equipment or cooked meals. The Docastaway team constantly monitors guests' safety, albeit from afar. "The goal is to allow castaways to not see people for one, two, three weeks. In isolation, you get to know yourself better. Once you know yourself better, you live better."

Another string to the bow of extreme travel, according to psychologist Sabine Sonnentag, is that it makes for a truly restorative vacation. She defines four pillars necessary for an effective holiday: relaxation, control, mastery experiences and mental detachment from work. While it may seem counterintuitive, survivor-esque experiences tick these boxes in a way that lying on a beach with an Aperol spritz never could.

In our age of 24/7 connectivity, the temptation to check in is ingrained. A study by Accountemps found that 62 per cent of workers aged 18 to 34 check in with the office while on annual leave. "Disconnecting while travelling has never been harder," explains Tom Marchant, the co-founder of Black Tomato, an award-winning creator of bespoke, immersive itineraries that span from Antarctica to the pathless wilds of Borneo. "The most meaningful changes happen when normality is taken out of the equation." That's why the company's pioneering Get Lost service places travellers in a remote, unknown territory, with a few survival supplies and a map dotted with check-in points. The rest is up to them.

> **66** Life is to be experienced... In isolation, you get to know yourself better. Once you know yourself better, you live better"

Replacing the stresses of high-pressure life with trials of endurance and intellect may seem like fighting fire with fire, but there's nothing quite like having to find food and shelter to make your inbox pale into insignificance. There's less care for who has climbed the highest mountain than what one returns having learned. Stepping outside our technological bubble, physical challenges engage our minds and motor skills in a way no screen can match. "In a world that rarely tests or pushes us in this way, just knowing you can is a major boost to self-esteem and confidence," says Craddock, whose clients undergo intensive survival training before braving the wild.

For record-breaking traveller Antonia Bolingbroke-Kent, extreme travel is an opportunity to explore untold stories. Her company Silk Road Adventures offers expeditions across remote areas of Tajikistan, Palestine, Pakistan and more, each designed to expand people's cultural awareness. "It's a really hard sell," she says. "The '-stan' suffix has a connotation of danger – it's always seen through the negative prism of the news." She recalls one American guest who quit her job and married another traveller after a life-changing motorbike trip across Afghanistan. Meanwhile, many visitors to the West Bank have become passionate about the Palestinian cause. "People's eyes are opened," Bolingbroke-Kent enthuses. "Our guests return home as ambassadors, spreading positivity about places with a high-risk image. It's an antidote to all the negative media."

Effects that linger post-travel give survivications their transformational edge over a purely experiential journey. Michael Bennett, co-founder of the Transformational Travel Council, has written a thesis examining the elements of adventure travel that lead to deep personal revolution. He identifies a "hero's journey" in which travellers venture into the unknown, face extraordinary challenges, learn from meaningful actions and reconnect with themselves, ultimately changing their lives upon their return home.

Knowledge. Broadened perspectives. Personal growth. Travel has become more extreme not because we crave danger, but because of the life-affirming opportunities it offers. Only by radically departing from the everyday can we cast off its excesses and recalibrate. Survivications are the travel industry's answer to a psychologist's couch. We may overcome challenges posed by the earth's unknown corners, but the greatest journey is the one towards ourselves.

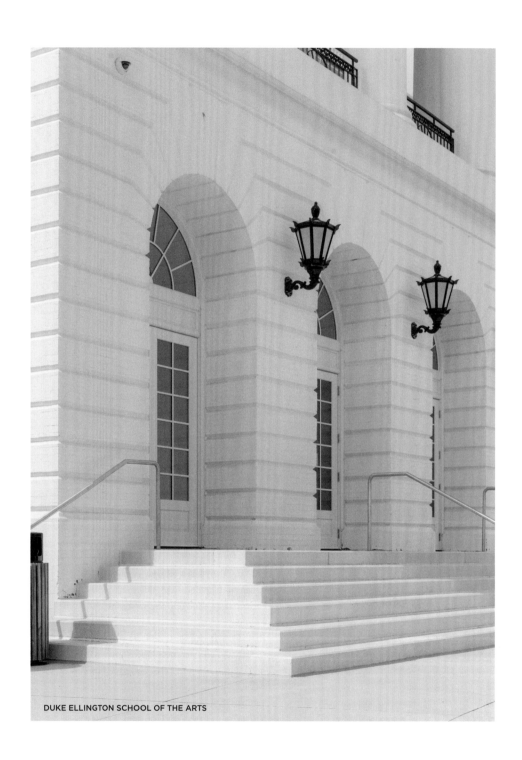

DUKE ELLINGTON SCHOOL OF THE ARTS

State of the Nation

It may be best known as the engine room of American politics, but **Washington DC** is also a city with its own drum to beat. And a new wave of artists, activists and entrepreneurs are making some noise

———

Words by **MOLLY MCARDLE**
Photos by **CERRUTI DRAIME**

You can see my old bedroom window from the sidewalk outside of Florida Avenue Grill. I point it out before we head inside the diner-style eatery, although it's been a decade since that window belonged to me – since I moved away from the city where I was born. Regardless, Washington DC is still home to me – its gently rising hills and thick canopy of trees, broad avenues and brick-row houses, heavy summer air and unselfconscious cosmopolitanism.

As world capitals go, however, few are as overshadowed by their governments as DC. It's not that people don't go – indeed, most Americans visit Washington DC on school or family trips – but their focus is usually federal. Think government buildings, national monuments and the city's enviable array of free museums. It's easy to get lost in this marble-clad core and forget the existence of the surrounding neighbourhoods, much less venture into them. But those who neglect the rest of DC are missing out on a great American city – one that hides in plain sight.

Florida Avenue Grill claims to be the oldest soul-food restaurant in the world. Founded in 1944, they may be right. But what comes off the griddle doesn't need history to recommend it – to me, it's still the best fried catfish in the world. The restaurant, lined with signed photos of local celebrities from Marion Barry (our infamous mayor) to Strom Thurmond (South Carolina's infamous senator), is one of the few places in the city that hasn't changed much in my lifetime. Since 2000 the city has experienced incredible growth – demographic, economic and otherwise – that has profoundly impacted its physical streetscape as well as the make-up of its population. This radical metamorphosis is not yet over, but while DC residents have long been asking who this change is for, a rising generation of artists, activists and entrepreneurs have begun to offer a new answer. ▶ ▶

"I really like DC so much," the Grammy-nominated, hip-hop artist Christylez Bacon confesses to me. He breaks down the charms of the city he's lived in his whole life. "It's a blend of fast-paced New York and also a chill, Southern type of vibe. I always say it's 'too south for the north, too north for the south'. It's in-between, a Goldilocks zone." Bacon's critically acclaimed concert series, Washington Sound Museum, combines progressive hip-hop with world music traditions from India to Brazil and Ireland to Senegal. When he and I were in high school together I watched him learn to play guitar on the bus to and from various field trips, a homemade slide on one finger as he teased out the intricacies of his instrument. Now he carries it with him on stage across the world, crisp in his signature suits and ascots (side note: he's also one of Washingtonian magazine's most stylish people). Yet even here he encounters people who are surprised he's from the city. "I catch that," he says, laughing. "Someone's like, 'What, a native?'". Bacon isn't angry, exactly, but he is a little incredulous. "Yeah, of course there are going to be people who are from here."

DC's cultural invisibility has real-world consequences. From his 14th-Street office Bo Shuff, the executive director of the non-profit advocacy organisation DC Vote, blames the conflation between the US federal government and the city it's located in. "The media often talk about Washington when they mean Congress," he explains. Yet ironically DC's close to 700,000 residents – a population greater than the rural states of Vermont and Wyoming – have no representation in Congress at all. Shuff's mission – to end the historic disenfranchisement of Washington residents who bear all of the responsibilities of a state but few of the rights – is bound up in language. Though media outlets may complain of "gridlock in Washington" and politicians boast of "draining the swamp", none are referencing problems created by actual Washingtonians. Instead they describe the 400-plus men and women (mostly men) sent here by the rest of the country to govern. Shuff's challenge is to tell the world that DC exists and that the people who live here matter.

The city Shuff wants to share is a place where art, activism and commerce blend. Poets open radical bookstores. Entrepreneurs become incubators. And everyone is an activist. Glimpses of this DC are visible throughout the city, from arts organisations like the Anacostia Playhouse and DC Artists East to businesses like the Spice Suite (activist Angel Anderson's heavenly smelling boutique), Busboys and Poets (perhaps the world's only poetry-themed restaurant group) and the DC branch of the Wing (the millennial-pink co-working space for women). However a persistent concern as the city grows is gentrification – and even erasure. A recent marketing campaign from a local glossy magazine advertised a line of T-shirts reading "I'm Not a Tourist, I Live Here". Yet not one of the models sporting them were black, even though black Washingtonians still represent the city's largest racial demographic. One of the organisers of a protest launched in response, the author Tony Lewis Jr, told a local radio station, "We aren't being included – and it's painful." ▶ ▶

FLORIDA AVENUE GRILL

DESIRÉE VENN FREDERIC

EATON WORKSHOP HOTEL

Although this concern is a very real one, as I criss-cross DC I notice that real-estate developers have become marginally better at fitting into existing streetscapes rather than razing them in order to rebuild from scratch. The new Wharf development along the southeast waterfront hugs but does not impede upon the Maine Avenue open-air fish market, the country's oldest and where Chesapeake blue crabs – both a regional delicacy and an obsession – are sold either live or steamed and with or without a thick coating of Old Bay seasoning. In the fast-developing Ivy City neighbourhood a striking former department-store warehouse has been transformed into condos rather than left empty or torn down. However, the small businesses that preceded these smart new developments still worry about their effects. Pia Carusone, the co-owner of Republic Restoratives Distillery where I sip bright apple brandy, wonders if they'll be able to afford their rent when the lease is up.

With this in mind I meet Desirée Venn Frederic, the former head of retail incubator Nomad Yard Collectiv, who now chairs the Local Merchant Independent Retail Association, a coalition of DC merchants and retailers that advocates for small business owners in local and federal legislation. Frederic's background in fashion retail is apparent: she's probably the best-dressed person on the block. She tells me that the Local Merchant Independent Retail Association was born of her concern for economic diversity. "Small businesses are being wiped out as a result of property tax increases," she explains. At the same time, she wouldn't say she's anti-development. "I do believe cities should improve. Cities are not museums – they cannot remain static. DC should be able to set the tone."

Our meeting place is the just-opened Eaton Workshop Hotel, a plush "activism-oriented" hotel on K Street, famous for its lobbying firms. Founded by Katherine Lo with the aim of becoming "the ultimate utopian gathering place" (and tagged by others as the first "anti-Trump hotel"), the Eaton cites a mix of inspiration including the Women's Marches and the Vietnam-era anti-war movement. Within its highly Instagrammable interiors I find a library lined with political-leaning literature by bell hooks and Jacqueline Woodson, a mural dedicated to civil rights activist Ruby Bridges and the Universal Declaration of Human Rights replacing the Bible on bedside tables. ▶▶

Although it looks the part, I'm initially sceptical about whether a hotel can change the world. However, Katherine tells me that the Eaton's ultimate ambition is to offer a "real platform for the community" – and with a cinema that will host film screenings and panel discussions, rooms where activists, campaigners and journalists can work for free and a nearby local members' club offering spaces for collaboration, it's clear she's made a real investment in physical spaces that can be of use to activist communities.

Meanwhile the food scene in DC has exploded, spearheaded in part by José Andrés and the introduction of a Michelin Guide, and restaurants both old and new are asking how they can better serve a changing city. Over in Georgetown, DC stalwart Guapo's has opened a new, upscale outpost of its greasy-spoon Mexican that pulls off the uncanny but undoubtedly successful merger of tradition and innovation. While the first Guapo's has "something any restaurant would envy – repeat customers", the Georgetown spot's manager admits to me, it's only the recent location's mezcal cocktails and artful ceviches that attract the new ones.

The city's food culture is dominated by fresh, exciting projects. At Himitsu, which serves brilliant south- and southeast Asian-inspired cuisine in an understated setting, co-founder Carlie Steiner says that she and her partner, James Beard-nominated chef Kevin Tien, want to offer an incubator for young people in the industry. Sitting inside the restaurant on a quiet street in Petworth, a neighbourhood which has seen considerable change, Steiner reflects: "You can't talk about new restaurants without talking about gentrification. How do you behave responsibly and still live out your dream of opening a new restaurant? We wouldn't be here if Petworth wasn't already cool, but coming here is also an important part of seeing DC." That dichotomy is "real DC", she adds.

On my last day in the city I make a pilgrimage to another part of DC integral to my past, as well as the city's future – the Duke Ellington School of the Arts. A glistening white building inside and out, it reopened in 2017 after a multi-year, multimillion-dollar renovation. "It's like being put in a stasis pod in the early 2000s and waking up way in the future," my old friend Bacon warns me. "You're like, 'What is this place?' It's like sci-fi." Itself an incubator, the school has produced some of DC's most widely celebrated artists, from comedian Dave Chappelle to actor Samira Wiley. I meet a class of young writers and filmmakers who tell me about growing up watching the city change around them. "We don't want to lose DC culture," one says, describing a documentary project they are in the midst of making. Despite the challenges ahead, when I look at them I can't help but think the city is in no danger.   ▶ ▶

STAY

EATON WORKSHOP HOTEL

1201 K STREET NW

eatonworkshop.com/hotel/dc

Rooms from £152

Hong Kong native Katherine Lo, the daughter of Langham hotel founder Lo Kah-shui, chose to locate the flagship of her new brand in downtown DC. The hotel-cum-activist space comes equipped with meeting rooms, a cinema, a digital radio booth and co-working offices, along with staff composed of veteran community organisers.

THE DARCY

1515 RHODE ISLAND AVENUE NW

thedarcyhotel.com

Rooms from £137

The Darcy offers up the hyperlocal in Logan Circle, having partnered with Ivy City's New Columbia Distillers, Arlington's Element Shrub, Connecticut Avenue tailor Read Wall and start-up Urban Flowers. Trusted chefs operate its two restaurants, Robert Wiedmaier's Michelin-star Siren and David Guas's New Orleans-inspired Lil'B Coffee Bar.

THE DARCY

EAT

BRESCA

1906 14TH ST NW

brescadc.com

Book ahead for a table at this Michelin-starred gem, where the burrata is light and the cocktails come in glasses shaped like giant bees. Bresca is also the only restaurant in DC to have joined the Zero Food Print Initiative, which helps restaurants and diners reduce their climate impact.

VACE ITALIAN DELICATESSEN

3315 CONNECTICUT AVENUE NW

vaceitaliandeli.com

Vace has enjoyed a cult following among Washingtonians since this little neighbourhood deli first opened in 1976. If you're not there to stock up on ravioli, grab a pizza slice (or a whole made-to-order pie) to go. Their particular, peculiar innovation? Cheese on the bottom, sauce on the top.

LE DIPLOMATE

1601 14TH STREET NW

lediplomatedc.com

This laundromat-turned-French bistro unites politicians and stylish locals alike (including Michelle Obama and Ivanka Trump) with its artful homage to Gallic café culture. The menu is of the macarons and oysters variety and its tables are always packed, so be sure to book in advance.

BRESCA

DO

UNION MARKET

1309 5TH STREET NE

unionmarketdc.com

Located in the rapidly developing NoMa neighborhood, Union Market is one of the best food halls in the country. Sample from a cornucopia of casual food and drink options or take home some kitchen supplies from one of several small retailers.

FREDERICK DOUGLASS HOUSE

1411 W STREET SE

nps.gov/frdo/index.htm

America's greatest abolitionist is celebrated as a Washingtonian by locals and a visit to his house, maintained by the National Park Service, is well worth it.

SUNDAY DRUM CIRCLE

MALCOLM X PARK, NEAR 16TH STREET AND CRESCENT PLACE NW

Legend states that the Malcolm X Drum Circle began spontaneously after the murder of the Muslim Civil Rights leader back when the park was still called Meridian Hill. As it has for over four decades, this weekly Sunday afternoon event begins at 3pm.

UNION MARKET

DRINK + DANCE

WICKED BLOOM

1540 NORTH CAPITOL STREET NW

wickedbloomdc.com

On Monday nights this rustic whiskey bar on the corner of North Capitol and Florida Avenue is the place to be for DC's queer women and non-binary folks of colour, with DJ MIM spinning an eclectic mix of music.

THE IVY ROOM

1369 NEW YORK AVE NE

republicrestoratives.com

Located within the Republic Restoratives distillery, The Ivy Room is a minimalist-feeling bar that proudly serves up its own brand of made-in-DC liquor.

BARMINI

501 9TH STREET NW

minibarbyjoseandres.com/barmini

José Andrés is the benevolent fairy godmother of DC dining, and Barmini – the molecular gastronomy-minded bar attached to his two-Michelin Minibar – is his magical laboratory.

BARMINI

Washington DC

Photographer: MITCH PAYNE
Stylist: TONA STELL

1. Tibi Alpaca Cosy Pullover Sweater in Heather Grey *£365*, **2. Loeffler Randall** Indy Circle Crossbody Bag in Nutmeg-Brown Croc-Embossed Leather *£414*, **3. Heath** Hair + Body Wash *£8*, **4. Clark's Botanicals** Cellular Lifting Moisture Mist *£45*, **5. YMC** Red Geanie Jean in Ecru *£165*, **6. Kronaby** Carat 38mm Gold Watch *£425*, **7. Carhartt** Great Master Shirt in Hamilton Brown *£85*

8. L'Officine Universelle Buly Savon Superfin Al Kassir *£25.50,* **9. Tom Daxon** Crushing Bloom Perfume in 100ml *£155,* **10. Aeydé** Lou Ankle Boots in Cognac Calf *£249,* **11. Sunspel** Cotton Loopback Sweatshirt in Archive White *£105,* **12. Sachajuan** Thickening Conditioner *£22,* **13. Sachajuan** Thickening Shampoo *£20,* **14. Perricone MD** Deep Crease Serum *£129*

Community Spirit

The founder of creative community Women Who asks if the new breed of global co-working/living concepts deliver on that elusive sense of belonging

———

Words by **OTEGHA UWAGBA**

As an author and speaker, I frequently have to travel internationally for work – words I can hardly believe I'm lucky enough to be typing. Work from anywhere – that's the millennial dream, right? These days it seems I can barely move for think pieces and business manuals extolling the virtues of "digital nomadism" – of jumping on a plane at a moment's notice, laptop in hand, and filing copy from the beach before moving on to another exotic locale, all while uploading a steady stream of photos to your Instagram feed that make the "normals" at home weep with jealousy. Yet few of these narratives properly address how lonely – and exhausting – that lifestyle can be when it's a regular feature of your working life.

Getting to travel is one of the aspects of my work that I value most, but it can also at times frustrate me to the point of tears. There's nothing like fighting for the last remaining charging point, propping up a melancholy restaurant table for one or struggling to tap into the local creative network to really take the sheen off arriving in a new city. However, where existing responses to life on the road may have failed, commerce perseveres, and a new breed of community spaces have sprung up with a view to catering to the work/travel woes of the entrepreneurial creative class.

Take Zoku, an Amsterdam-based "work-meets-play" concept that is part hotel, part apartment and part co-working space and which launched into the public consciousness by proudly declaring "The End of The Hotel Room". Co-founders Marc Jongerius and Hans Meyer – the latter a founding partner of hotel chain citizenM – attribute Zoku's secret sauce to "building a genuine human connection between guests and "Sidekicks" (the Zoku term for community managers) upon arrival, and solving their biggest challenges when they arrive in a city they might not know, in a country in which they might not speak the language."

Admittedly, its minimalist branding and stripped pine interiors can feel a tiny bit off-putting, given that when I travel for work I'm usually looking for accommodation that feels like a home away from home – there's a lot to be said for a cosy-looking sofa and dim lighting. However, the Sidekicks that roam Zoku's communal spaces facilitating member introductions via workshops and dinners counteract the futuristic aesthetic, integrating travellers into the community and helping them get their bearings as quickly as possible.

Then there's Roam, a co-living and co-working space with a slightly wider footprint than Zoku and locations in Miami, Bali, Tokyo and San Francisco. While undoubtedly worthwhile as holiday destinations, few of their bases are in the key cities where creatives – and therefore work – tend to congregate, making me question just how practical a Roam membership would be. However, perhaps I'm overlooking the appeal of a truly nomadic

working life. I'm put in touch with one of their members, or "Roamers" as the company calls them (which as a method of creating a sense of shared identity is surely the oldest trick in the book). Kristina Barger, a 37-year-old cognitive scientist, uses Roam so she can travel freely and consult around the world, with her longest Roam stint to date lasting three months. Currently between London and Amsterdam, she first discovered Roam when she was setting up a base in London.

She cites the networking opportunities on offer and the ability to cultivate genuine friendships as part of Roam's appeal. "I've met some really interesting people who are now great friends, and whom I expect to be so for life. That might sound suspect, but the intimacy level at Roam is higher because you encounter people more often and in more varied scenarios than just at work or in your

daily life – so you can connect on a more emotional level. There've been Roam romances." I'm initially amused by that last comment, but given the ambitions many of these businesses harbour of catering to every aspect of our waking lives, it doesn't seem that implausible that they might one day incorporate dating services into their models – even if that does carry a touch of Black Mirror.

Barger touches on something significant though, specifically the importance of face-to-face contact and connecting with real people in real time. In a world dominated by digital tools and interfaces, it's easy to be fooled into thinking we're connecting with others – or even part of a community – while actually being physically alone. Both Roam and Zoku exist squarely at the creative tech start-up intersection that so many young urban professionals (please don't call us yuppies)

▲
ABOVE

The interior of
Zoku in Amsterdam
*Photo by Ewout Huibers
for Zoku and concrete*

have come to recognise as part of the 21st-century formulation of work. They're cut from the same cloth as early iterations of WeWork, with plenty of talk about "disruption" and "co-creation" – Zoku's co-founders actually describe their model to me as "always beta", which... okay.

At the other end of the spectrum is Norn, a members' club with bases in London and Berlin. More intimate and homespun than either Roam or Zoku, its spaces are really just (large) residential houses with several bedrooms, and founder Travis Hollingsworth is clearly striving for a more cerebral atmosphere than Norn's more corporate competitors. Their signature event is the Conversation Dinner, where guests are served a series of topical prompts in-between courses, a format no doubt designed to evoke the literary sophistication of 18th-century European salons – previous themes have included youth and karma.

Visiting their (since closed) Barcelona base in the sticky heat of the Mediterranean summer for one such event, I attended a dinner comprised of 15 or so strangers, ending up deep in conversation with a born-again Christian skater who quizzed me about my relationship with my parents. The evening was certainly thought-provoking, though I can't help but wonder whether it's the sort of event I'd want to attend on a regular basis as opposed to experiencing as a one-off.

Still, if there's one thing I noticed during my week-long stay at Norn Barcelona, it was that I got things done. Months of plodding along with a long-overdue book proposal were brought to a gratifying conclusion and I finalised the remaining third in a matter of days, sitting in the cool shade of a fig tree that overlooked the terrace, pausing only to nibble on perfectly ripe nectarines purchased from the local frutería.

So what does one need to consider when building a co-living, co-working space? What are the ideal conditions for an authentic community to take root and prosper? Well, there's the practical stuff, which so many seem to get wrong. You need a designated workspace with actual desks, because there's only so long you can spend cross-legged and hunched over your laptop on a sofa or sunlounger. You also need clear divisions between a space's work, social and living zones. While Zoku's model of "hybrid living", where one lives and works in the same space, sounds great – or at least effective – on paper I suspect the reality of staying there might be that one never really switches off. As a self-employed person whose life is an increasingly interwoven hybrid of social, work and leisure time, these days I crave distinctions between those three arenas wherever possible. Finally, it's important to keep things simple. Though it might sound appealing to include every amenity under the sun, install a ping-pong table or splash out on a hot tub, in reality

I've found the places I've worked best from when travelling – from hotel rooms to co-working spaces to rented villas – have been comfortable but free of distractions, no matter how well-intended.

What's hardest to manufacture – and the greatest challenge for this new breed of live-work spaces – are the softer measures, the intangibles that make one feel a genuine sense of community. A robust way of responding to and incorporating user feedback, for example, so members feel they have a voice, or making members feel invested enough to become active participants in community life, because nothing kills a community faster than passive members. Indeed, what about allowing members to make connections with each other independently of a central organising figure (which to many businesses veers scarily close to risking obsolescence)? Nail that and you've got a billion-dollar concept on your hands.

THE LOWDOWN

ZOKU
From £133 per night, which drops to around £89 per night for stays of a month upwards
livezoku.com

ROAM
Price varies by location, starting from £380 per week (£1,370 per month) and going up to £912 per week (£3,195 per month)
roam.co

NORN
Local membership (events only) £374 per year; residency membership (living on-site) £1,495 per month
norn.co

Hope and Homecoming

Lebanon's capital of **Beirut** is reaching back to its
"Paris of the Middle East" past through a fresh generation
of native diaspora and refugee newcomers

———

Words by **BEX HUGHES**
Photos by **ABBI KEMP**

As I propel north through Beirut from the city's airport I pass battered suburbs, ageing apartment blocks and sandstone monoliths. Creeping into the centre, the number of JG Ballard-esque, high-rise developments increases. Like many cities, Beirut is in a state of metamorphosis. Unlike most, the marks of recent ferocious conflict are everywhere. Lebanon's civil war lasted from 1975 until 1990 and left gaping holes in the country's population, mirrored by the pockmarks of sniper bullets and bomb blasts in its tranquil leafy streets.

Today the city is on the move – but for our host, Samer Ghorayeb, the preservation of Beirut's past is a concern. "Fifteen years ago," he tells us, "there were 1,300 protected buildings in this city. Now there are around 200." Government-supported construction companies requisition and develop damaged buildings and empty plots around the city and more often than not the real estate holds infinitely more value without a bombed-out, dilapidated palace atop it. Samer's own commitment to preservation finds form in Baffa House, a 1940s building that mixes Ottoman and European architectural styles with high ceilings, tiled floors and airy French windows, all bathed in that oh-so-lovely Mediterranean light. Lived in by his grandparents – the house is named for his Italian-immigrant grandfather Antonio Baffa – Samer kickstarted the building's substantial renovation and reopened it as a guesthouse in 2014. For myself and photographer Abbi, both based in Dubai and used to desert-scapes and "executive" skyscrapers, it's nothing less than disparate bliss.

Baffa House is riding a wave. After years of political uncertainty and security concerns, Beirut's tourist industry and small businesses are once again in bloom. Samer tells us that diaspora Lebanese are returning to the city, some gone as long as three generations and from all corners of the globe. He is cautiously hopeful but the situation is still far from straightforward. Lebanon's patchwork demographic includes sizeable communities of Palestinians who have settled here since the 1948 Palestine War. There has also been a substantial influx of Syrians into the country since the start of Syria's civil war in 2011. The country's map of ethnic groups and religious denominations – Armenian and Druze, Muslim and Christian – is labyrinthine. Presided over by a Maronite Christian President, a Sunni Muslim Prime Minister and a Shi'i Muslim Head of Parliament, politics are often in deadlock. The Shi'a political organisation Hezbollah garners strong support in certain areas of Lebanon, including Beirut's southern suburbs, providing public services where the government has failed. ▶▶

ACHRAFIEH

SOUK EL TAYEB FARMERS' MARKET

As a result Samer's guesthouse retains a healthy dose of nostalgia for the era of his grandparents in the 1950s, 1960s and 1970s, a golden pre-war period of peace. Samer still owns pieces of their well-loved furniture and photos of happy days gone by are enshrined on the walls. His mother, Diva, makes the breakfast preserves and a dairy-free saffron cake called Sfouf, an accidental vegan masterpiece and an ingenious answer to electricity shortages and unreliable refrigerators during the war. Images by his brother, the photographer Jad Ghorayeb, and his aunt, the renowned contemporary artist Laure Ghorayeb, line the walls. Laure's works also hang in the Sursock Museum, a contemporary Lebanese art museum in the next-door Achrafieh neighbourhood that Abbi and I visit after a Baffa breakfast of champions. Born in 1931 and still creating, Laure's frenzied mixed-media collages and stark, surreal paintings confront heritage, war and violence with a dark, humorous energy. In two of her collages she has decorated images of long-gone ancestors and divisive Lebanese politicians with baubles, string, cartoons and childlike scribbles.

This energy is a common theme in modern Beirut, where imagination and a hunger for change spring from a thorny past. At Souk el Tayeb, a Beirut-based co-operative, founder Kamal Mouzawak aims to soothe his fractured nation one meal at a time. Kamal started the Souk el Tayeb farmers' market in 2004 for producers from all of Lebanon's regions, religions and ethnic groups to come together to bring soul food to the city. Nearly 100 producers are now involved in the effort, with all profits going directly back into the production process. Souk el Tayeb's simple message of good food and goodwill has now mushroomed into five guesthouses, seven restaurants and training schemes for migrant workers and underprivileged refugee women.

In a leafy enclave off Mar Mikhael's Armenia Street lies Tawlet Souk el Tayeb, the organisation's Beirut restaurant. There are five menu changes a week here, each cooked by a chef from a different region of the country with their own distinct versions of fattoush, kibbeh and other Lebanese staples.

Before a lunch cooked by Nada from Lebanon's eastern Bekaa Valley (where the fertile ground produces much of the country's wine, vegetables and dairy), we settle into a light-filled corner with Hana, Tawlet's manager. "Lebanon has a lot of ideologies when it comes to religion and politics," she tells us. "People are very conflicted. There's always been war and differences that have torn people apart. The only thing we have in common is our food, the produce, the land we create it from." She also quietly reveals that many of Souk el Tayeb's makers and chefs have deeply touching stories related to Lebanon's traumatic past. "It's nice to see that out of all this heartbreak we're creating a sense of home."

Hana joined Souk el Tayeb after an education abroad and an unsatisfying corporate job, following the increasing current of diaspora Lebanese returning to the country. "I felt like I needed to give back – these people represent my family, my ideology... Lebanese are fed up with the plateau, politics, economy. The new generation is trying to create more change so that people can have hope." She describes a craving for patriotism from Lebanon's young: "You'll see a lot of places around Beirut hinting towards the 1960s and 1970s – that was the time when Beirut was known as the 'Paris of the Middle East', when it was lively, it was beautiful. My parents and grandparents talk about that time as if it was a dream. We're trying to bring that back." ▶▶

DOWNTOWN BEIRUT

SOUK EL TAYEB FARMERS' MARKET

MAR MIKHAEL

CREATIVE SPACE

CORNICHE

Leaving Tawlet, we tread west through the city through elegant residential streets to Beirut's downtown, home of Creative Space Beirut (CSB). A social enterprise providing free fashion design education, CSB is the brainchild of Sarah Hermez. Born to Lebanese parents, Sarah grew up in Kuwait and studied at New York's Parsons School of Design and the Eugene Lang College of Liberal Arts. "I wanted to come back to Lebanon to give something back – and to combine my passions for social justice and fashion," she explains. "There's no quality design education here and at CSB we believe that fostering talent helps a country to grow." With the support of friends and her co-founder Caroline Simonelli (Sarah's professor from Parsons, who still travels from the US to teach courses each year), CSB was born in 2011. Courses include fashion history, concept, design, sewing and business skills, and applications are open to all who reside in the country, be they Lebanese, Palestinian or Syrian. Sarah explains that the school funds itself through grants, tireless networking, events and three in-house brands – CSB Ready To Wear, Second St and Roni Helou, himself a 2016 graduate who'll be showcasing his designs at London's Somerset House in February 2019 as part of the International Fashion Showcase.

CSB has recently relocated to donated premises in the downtown Beirut Souks, bringing life to a largely empty modern development. Three years of intense study and a small number of pupils has formed a close-knit group and many graduates return to work alongside the students when they can. We gatecrash a late lunch where graduate Ahmed and second-year student Najah share their food and enthusiasm. Ahmed is currently working on his own brand – a Japanese-inspired line of T-shirts, abayas and cardigans – while Najah combines her studies with working at a hospice. "I was at work one day," she explains, "and I saw Sarah's TED Talk [a 2015 speech given at TEDxBeirut]. I applied just like that". While they'd like international reach, both students want to remain based in Lebanon. "CSB is a great opportunity," Ahmed

says. "It's an incentive to stay at home and work hard." For Najah, Sarah's enthusiasm for Lebanon is an inspiration. "She thought about her home country and how much it needs – the people who are thirsty to express their talents but don't have the means."

The evening sweeps us from CSB along the Beirut Corniche into Hamra, a frenetic neighbourhood in the west of the city. We feast on Beiruti Almaza beer, halloumi and tabbouleh at T'Marbouta, a favoured haunt of students (the American University of Beirut is a few minutes' walk away) hidden behind Hamra's main drag. Then we go underground. Tucked away in the basement of an unassuming Hamra shopping centre, Metro Al Madina is a hyper-funked, neon homage to an hedonistic Beirut of decades past. Formed in 2012 by a collective of artists, actors and musicians led by Hisham Jaber, this small-but-mighty venue is a fixed star in Beirut's performance scene. Staples include Hishik Bishik and Bar Farouk, hectic tributes to Egyptian and Lebanese cabaret culture through the decades. There's a constant stream of fresh acts and musical concerts, with "Midnight Metro" resident DJs powering the venue from – you guessed it – midnight on Fridays and Saturdays.

We settle into plush velvet seats for an evening of Koudoud Halabiya, a form of classical-folk music originating from the Syrian city of Aleppo. There's a heavy presence of Beiruti Syrians in the audience bantering back and forth with the group's singer and his ensemble, who play an assortment of traditional string and percussive instruments. The mood of the room rises and falls as the music swells from celebration to mourning. The catharsis of Koudoud Halabiya to the citizens of a war-torn homeland is potent – and nowhere understands that better than Beirut. Many threads make up the city's story, from European immigrants to its Armenian, Palestinian and Syrian diaspora, war-sick generations to returning expatriates. Yet from this chaos a modern, incomparable Beirut stands proud. ▷▷

STAY

VILLA CLARA

RUE KENCHAARA, ASHRAFIEH

villaclara.fr

Rooms from £154

The duck-egg blue façade of this 1920s townhouse is impossible to miss, tucked away as it is on a quiet side-street in the Mar Mikael area. There's a romantic belle époque vibe with Murano chandeliers, traditional tile floors and patterned wallpaper, while the hotel's restaurant serves up gourmet French dishes cooked by co-owner Olivier Gougeon.

BEIT EL TAWLET

ARMENIA STREET, MAR MIKHAEL

soukeltayeb.com/beit-el-tawlet

Rooms from £91

Souk el Tayeb's eight-bedroom guesthouse has 1960s- and 1970s-inspired decor and offers fantastic views of the city. Check out wholesome delights from Lebanese producers at its market or head to its restaurant for soul food made by chefs from each corner of the country. Post-meal nap essential.

BAFFA HOUSE

PATRIARCHE ARIDA STREET, MAR MIKHAEL

baffahouse.com

Rooms from £91

This authentic, plant-filled Lebanese family home has been lovingly restored by Samer Ghorayeb, his wife Jessica and their two small boys and offers a beautifully designed destination in the eastern Mar Mikhael neighbourhood, as well as unbeatable breakfasts and peace in the heart of the city.

BAFFA HOUSE

EAT

SEZA

PATRIARCH ARIDA, MAR MIKHAEL

+961 1 570 711

Armenian food served in an atmospheric family-run joint in the centre of Mar Mikhael. The oh-so-romantic garden is the perfect place to eat, drink and natter away an evening (a venerated Beiruti pastime) and the Armenian interiors game is strong.

MOTHERSHUCKER

NICHOLAS TURK STREET, MAR MIKHAEL

mothershucker.me

Oysters, gin and the best name in town. If you're not a fan of its shelled delights there's a sashimi bar – and if you're not a fan of that, there are knock-out cocktails to keep you happy. Open until 2am for that late-night seafood fix.

ABOU HASSAN

MAR YOUSSEF STREET, BOURJ HAMMOUD

+961 1 266 888

No-fuss Lebanese hummus, fresh-baked bread and foul (stewed beans with lemon and herbs). In a world of wannabes, Abou Hassan's hummus is the real deal. After a night out in the nearby nightclubs of B018 and Discotek, its version with spiced lamb will tempt the most sincere of "clean eaters".

T'MARBOUTA

HAMRA SQUARE CENTRE, HAMRA

+961 1 350 274

This spot, beloved of American University of Beirut students, has good-value grub, cold beer and its very own library. Keep your eyes peeled for its unassuming entrance in a shopping-centre facade. Tucked out back is a colourful, cosy secret garden.

LEBANESE BAKERY

SALIM BUSTROS STREET, ACHRAFIEH

thelebanesebakery.com

A Lebanese flatbread (manousheh) paradise – try it sweet, savoury or every-which-way. The joint is owned by brothers Samer and Bassam Chamoun – Samer worked as an architect with the late, great Zaha Hadid – and a London branch has recently opened in Covent Garden.

DO

CHICO RECORDS
SADAT-SIDANI INTERSECTION, HAMRA
+961 1 743 855

Feted as the oldest record shop in Beirut and founded by Khatchik Mardirian, the father of current owner Diran, Chico has served up musical delectations since the 1960s and through war, peace and everything in-between.

METROPOLIS CINEMA
MICHEL BUSTROS, ACHRAFIEH
metropoliscinema.net

A luscious art-house cinema – the first and only in Lebanon – with a focus on Lebanese and Arabic films. The Metropolis hosts various events and festivals throughout the year as well as pop-ups across the country.

SURSOCK MUSEUM
GREEK ORTHODOX ARCHBISHOPRIC STREET, ASHRAFIEH
sursock.museum

Set in a street of equally awesome palatial piles, this early 20th-century, ornate villa houses an impressive collection of modern and contemporary Lebanese art, as well as international and Islamic art pieces.

BEIT BEIRUT
INDEPENDENCE STREET, SODECO
beitbeirut.org

A renovation of a traditional Lebanese family home devastated during the Civil War. Beit Beirut was intended for use as a cultural museum to commemorate the war, but as of October 2018 opening hours are irregular. Check before visiting.

SURSOCK MUSEUM

DRINK + DANCE

B 018
KARANTINA
+961 3 810 618

Chances are if you've heard anything about Beirut's nightlife, it's that there's a club in a bomb bunker. While that's not strictly true (B 018 was constructed in the late 1990s as an architectural response to the war), this club is certainly one of the city's icons.

METRO AL MADINA
SAROULLA CENTRE, HAMRA
metromadina.com

Performance wonderland in a shopping centre. Book in advance for shows or join from midnight on weekends for post-show DJ sets. There's a "metro station" bar in the foyer and bow-tied waiters dash between candlelit tables to keep you fuelled.

TORINO EXPRESS
RUE GOURAUD, GEMMAYZEH
+961 3 611 101

Set into the vaulted ground floor of an Ottoman-era building, this bar-of-bars serves up strong espressos and no-fills drinks to an arty local crowd. In the evening one corner transforms into a hole-in-the-wall DJ booth, pouring funk out into the street.

ABOU ELIE
KUWAIT STREET, KARAKAS
+961 70 918 821

Every day is a revolution in Abou Elie, where communist memorabilia from Mao to Che covers all surfaces. This one-of-a-kind speakeasy is named after its founder, a former Lebanese Communist Party fighter.

METRO AL MADINA

Only Connect

A legacy of photographic storytelling
that reaches through history into our
shared humanity

———

Words by **ANNABEL NUGENT**
Photos by **STEVE MCCURRY**

Deeply visceral and undeniably emotive, the photographer Steve McCurry's images are the antithesis of the objectivity that his craft often relies on. Instead he chooses to pull focus on to the faces of war-torn regions, injecting a humanity into the statistics and numerical figures that scroll across the ticker tape of the six o'clock news.

In Steve McCurry: A Life in Pictures: 40 Years of Photography, McCurry's sister Bonnie weaves together her brother's personal notes, telegrams and unpublished images to tell the stories behind both his most seminal and more obscure photographs and the subjects they portray. The book is a rare divulgence of McCurry's work, usually captioned with only a location and date.

In 1979, disguised in local attire and without a passport, McCurry was smuggled into Afghanistan just before the Soviet invasion closed the country to all western journalists. He later returned to Pakistan with rolls of film sewn into his clothes and delivered the first photographic evidence of the conflict. Since then he has continued to venture into "government unadvisable" regions, crossing national borders in order to transcend cultural ones.

McCurry's work locates the personal within the political. "When I have a strong emotional reaction to a particular situation, I always try to show the story of how those people live their lives," he says. "I want to have some sort of insight into the human condition of the subject." Nowhere is this intent more apparent than in McCurry's portraits, the penetrating green-eyed glare of the Afghan Girl (Sharbat Gula) having become embedded into our collective consciousness as a symbol of the plight of refugees around the world.

As he did with the mujahideen in 1979, McCurry believes "it's important to fully immerse yourself in the lives of your subjects. You have to break down barriers to create a sense of comfort and photograph people with a sympathetic and empathetic eye in order to tell their story effectively." Through this respectful approach he captures serendipitous moments such as a man selling oranges from the bonnet of his car, a young girl leaning out of a window or a mother with a baby on her hip. These universal expressions of humanity connect "how those people live their lives" with how his audience lives theirs, revealing a shared humanity which does not abide by physical borders or language.

"I want to show people's humanity in whatever situation they find themselves. Children have a universal need to play whether they live in a bombed-out building, a hut or a comfortable home. I've photographed children playing on tanks, in graveyards, in the streets and in parks. I find that laughing, smiling and having a sense of humour are universal," McCurry says. It is this happiness that shines through his work and is often most affecting.

The photographer acknowledges that "finding positivity is not something you consciously look for. When photographing you're drawn to certain situations instinctively and I'm always amazed by the resilience and optimism people have despite extreme poverty and privation. I've learnt that there is a commonality among people, whatever their country or nationality, and that people want to be respected wherever they are in the world. If you can respect people, it's a wonderful world – doors open up."

"Connecting with people has never been so essential to protect our humanity," he continues – and in a time when immigration rhetoric is too often dehumanising and questions of representation are being debated, McCurry's work in showing the humanity of faraway issues is more pertinent than ever.

Steve McCurry: A Life in Pictures: 40 Years of Photography (2018) by Bonnie McCurry, published by Laurence King

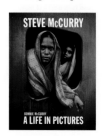

Rajasthan, India, 1983

Peshawar, Pakistan, 1984

Maimana, Afghanistan, 1992

Baluchistan, Pakistan, 1981

Maimana, Afghanistan, 2003

Sana'a, Yemen, 1997

Srinagar, Kashmir, 1995

Hajjah, Yemen, 1999

Treasure Island

An easy narrative eludes our Digital Editor-in-Chief in an off-grid, off-road expedition through untouched **Madagascar**, where nomadic forest tribes still thwart the hungry reach of tourism

―――――

Words by **INDIA DOWLEY**
Photos by **MARK LEAVER**

I can't tell you a story about Madagascar. Stories have a beginning, a middle and an end. There tends to be some sort of message in them and a clear trajectory towards uncovering it. But the days I spent on this island nation adrift off the coast of Mozambique cannot be chronicled or distilled. They are a matryoshka doll of tales, a patchwork of encounters.

Most destinations come with a preformed narrative that shapes your expectations – you've read the bumf, seen photographs plastered all over Instagram and your colleague visited last year. However, I had few preconceptions of Madagascar. Unlike Kenya with safaris or Bali with beaches, it has not been neatly pre-packaged for tourists but is instead raw, rough around the edges and unabashedly true to itself. As a result, I find myself clumsily clutching at memories: there is no map on which to plot my coordinates or skeleton on which to hang my words.

Much to the disappointment of family and friends, spotting a lemur was not my raison d'être. I wanted to peer behind the curtain of exotic mysticism that I'd cloaked upon this foot-shaped landmass since childhood, when I'd sat on my bedroom floor and traced its outline on my precious globe. Our trip was curated by Natural World Safaris, which specialises in places that have not yet been manicured for the masses – the last blank spaces, the final frontiers. As such, Mark and I spend a week picking our way along the south-west coast, leaving the luxurious hotels in the north to wildlife tourists and diving fanatics in favour of taking the road less travelled (and often no road at all, such is the embryonic state of the country's infrastructure).

It begins in the capital, Antananarivo (affectionately known as "Tana"), a frenetic and peculiar hotchpotch in which French-colonial houses jostle for space alongside shacks with corrugated-iron roofs. Chalkboard signs inscribed with foie gras, quiche lorraine and beef bourguignon are juxtaposed with glowing cabinets of street food crammed with oily beige parcels. Rickshaws, motorbikes and VW Beetles choke and snort their way along the one stretch of tarmac leading into the centre. It's Friday evening rush hour and the city is chomping at the bit to get home. ►►

We join them, dancing a disjointed hop along a pavement of shattered concrete, ditches and drainage holes that serve as a reminder of the heavy rainfall that baptises this tropical land. We take a side road – it opens onto a serene rice paddy and suddenly we're in Southeast Asia. We take another and the sweet smell of raw meat catches in my throat – we've stumbled into a night market and an impressive display of glistening ruby-red flesh is suspended from hooks before me. I lose Mark in the darkened rows of stalls and feel the effervescent thrill of being alone in a strange place. There are no tourists here. The smell of charcoal clings to the evening air. Goosebumps spring up on my arms. It's only been a matter of hours, but Madagascar has already got under my skin.

A 50-minute flight from east to west reveals a Martian panorama of burnt ochre-red folds, a scorched, earthy plane reminiscent of my bronzer palette. It's a terrain so alien that my mind plays tricks on me – I swear I see plumes of smoke rising off the ground, hissing and spitting in greeting as we swoop down to land. We're in Morondava for the mighty baobab trees, the only real "sight" on our Madagascar hit list, and we race straight to the "Avenue des Baobabs" from the airport, desperate to arrive before sunset. Monstrously elegant, the fabled trees stand at over 30m tall and remind me of a toddler's plump arm topped by tiny, stubby fingers. I wonder who else has gazed upon their transcendent enormity: those first settlers who pitched up in outrigger canoes, pioneers in pirogues, or the pirates who followed in search of vanilla, gold and diamonds. Told that it would bring us good fortune, we place our hands on a handsome trunk as a sun the colour of a neon raspberry kisses the ground goodnight.

Back on the road, this time in a spine-rattling 4x4 that brings us along the coast to Belo sur Mer, a tiny town and commune that is cut off from the mainland for up to five months during rainy season. The sand and rock passageway is looked after by inhabitants of the villages we pass through and is in such poor condition that 25km takes over an hour. When navigating a particularly large bump I whack my head so hard on the window that the driver emergency stops, thinking we've collided with a boulder. A steely shard of black lacquer darts across our path and back into the undergrowth – a snake trying to escape the midday heat. I feel like I've reached the edge of the earth.

Our lodgings are the enchanting beachfront Hôtel Entremer, run by retired French novelist Laurence and her husband Alain. The six thatched cottages dotted among the palm trees and bougainvillea are all dark wood, four-poster beds and fluttering white canopies, with furniture for "sitting, reading, writing or dreaming" scattered with ephemera collected on the couple's travels, such as nautical maps and a mammoth malachite ashtray picked up in the Congo. Water is heated in glass bottles left to simmer in the sunshine while the bottles that line the bar are filled with homemade rum infused with every flavour – baobab, mandarin, raisin and, of course, vanilla. I want to taste them all, but we tear ourselves away to the sea. ▶▶

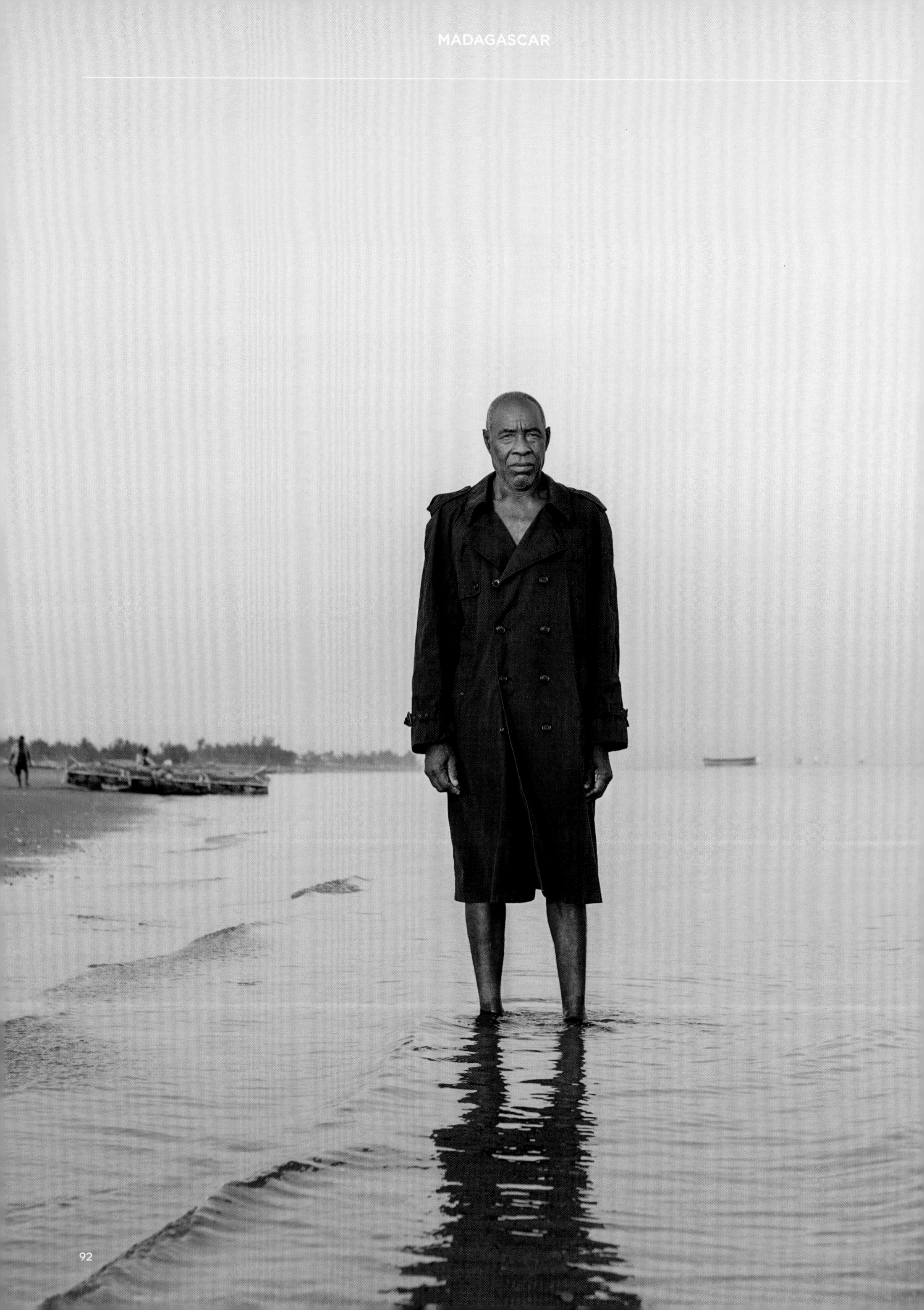

We walk for several hours, stopping to skim a stone, watch fishermen deftly removing squid ink from creatures with tentacles longer than my arm, and shake the hands of the scores of children who scamper down the beach to greet us. I devote a lot of time to crowd control while Mark tries to take photographs. People are kind and curious and no one tries to peddle us a pair of knock-off sunglasses – that sort of thing doesn't happen here, yet. Over a supper of crab salad and pineapple tarte tatin I learn that there are few jobs in Madagascar. There are a small number of eye-wateringly wealthy people, mainly in vanilla exportation (Madagascar is responsible for 80 per cent of the world's produce), but most live sustainably by fishing or working the land and sex work is not uncommon. The few who do put themselves through university often find themselves returning to live traditionally due to a lack of opportunities. Tourism would be a golden ticket for many, and I feel guilty for wanting Madagascar to stay just as it is.

Another day and this time we're on a boat. Our arrival couldn't have been less clandestine – we're met by an ever-expanding throng of children screeching with inquisitive mirth as they skip along the beach. I feel like some sort of reticent dignitary disembarking from a maiden voyage. Mark and I exchange sheepish looks. "Salama, salama!" ("I'm fine, I'm fine!") they cry out to us – the efficient Malagasy greeting that reflects an attitude of just getting on with things.

I've read that Morombe is a ghost town, a shell of a port abandoned by its inhabitants due to a lack of work, dilapidated, godforsaken, ruled by stray dogs and mosquitoes. I'm not convinced the author ever visited. The sky is the pink of sugared almonds, the sea flat and shimmering like the scales of a fish. Beautiful hand-carved, hand-painted pirogues with stitched-together sails that remind me of Battenberg cake are returning with the catch of the day and women with colourful baskets on their heads saunter down to meet them, faces daubed in mustard-hued paint (a natural sunscreen). A child is having a tantrum, lying on the sand face down while beating his clenched fists and refusing to move. I smile at the familiarity of this scene in such a foreign place and wander over to a group of men sitting cross-legged on the sand, laughing and puffing away while threading a mammoth fishing net. In garbled French I exchange pleasantries with Etienne, a jovial figure who claims to be 150 years old. His gnarled fingers are surprisingly nimble and he tells me with a wink that he'll complete the net in a matter of days. There's a real sense of industry here, as if everybody is toiling away and playing a part in sustaining their little kingdom.

Omelette stuffed into soft bread rolls and thick, black coffee sweetened with local honey are our deckside fuel as we kiss goodbye to Morombe, flying fish dancing around our boat. We're only travelling 100km south, though our trip takes almost five hours due to our repeated requests to stop so we can swim in the warm, duck-egg-blue waters. We could be in the Maldives and I can't believe the long stretches of completely empty ▶ ▶

coastline – not a hotel in sight – punctuated only by pop-up nomadic villages teetering on the periphery of civilisation. I watch as the landscape changes once again, becoming a pale chalky shade with trees the colour of jade – now we're in the Aegean. We make a pit stop to visit mangroves and try our hand at sailing a pirogue. I pick up some old fishing twine on the beach and wonder what Etienne is doing, then find a swirly mauve and mother-of-pearl shell and thread it on to make a bracelet. Mark and I have become competitive beachcombers, gawping at sea anemones the size of dessert plates, giant electric-red starfish that look like they've been plucked out of Finding Nemo and, most astonishingly, a gargantuan, shield-like turtle shell that comes up to my waist and is so pristine it looks like its inhabitant has simply swum out of it.

Mikea. As with every new place we arrive at, Mark and I head straight out along the beach, aiming for a settlement we've seen from the water. After about 45 minutes we arrive in a village that's all mud and wattle houses, gently smoking fires, goats scampering along with children and boats galore. Of course, yet again there's zero hope of going incognito and we're immediately mobbed by children with whom we spend an hour or so, placating them with photographs and candy-covered peanuts before finally taking exhausted refuge in a building labelled "La Discotheque". But being underage in a club isn't a thing in this not-so-sleepy fishing village and we're thwarted when the children pour in behind us, immediately slipping into a synchronised dance routine, air guitars out in force.

The chiselled proprietor, Robert, throws us an apologetic smile and plonks two beers before us. Then it's vanilla-laced rum with warm Fanta. Sweet inebriation engulfs me – barefoot and salty-skinned in this dreamlike pocket of the world, nothing has ever tasted so good. Robert looks on, inquisitive, bemused, protective. He's never had tourists in his bar. Despite repeated assurances that we're fine, he persuades his sister to cook for us and an hour or so later leads us to one of the rush dwellings I've been longing to be "organically" invited into. We're ushered behind a curtain, where an immaculately set table has been laid with fish in rich tomato sauce, a mountain of fluffy white rice and a singular flower. Robert bows and leaves us to it – we scoff the lot off chipped enamel plates, gulping down hot rice water (a staple of Malagasy meals) before staggering home in a cloud of contentment where we are berated by the hotel staff, who are about to send out a search party. They're not used to guests like us.

Comeuppance for our indulgence comes in the form of the next day's transport, a seatbelt-less buggy which I drive exactly how you'd imagine someone who wrote off a car in her second lesson to. We're off to meet the Mikea people, a nomadic group of hunter-gatherers who are widely regarded as mythical Vazimba, the very first inhabitants of Madagascar (though there is no evidence to support this). So cut off from the outside world are they that many Malagasy people don't believe they actually exist. I'm dubious and imagine some forced re-enactment including a "traditional" tribal dance before being coerced into purchasing gaudy souvenirs that I won't know what to do with when I get home. Scepticism has always been my friend and foe. ▶▶

After enduring three kilometres of being facially chastised by branches as we weave through the trees we become foot soldiers and thrash our way through deciduous thicket. Naya, our guide, pauses to listen every so often – I feel like we're tracking a wild animal and it makes me somewhat uneasy, but he assures me that he has been gradually fostering a relationship with the Mikea for years and they will be happy to meet us. Just as I begin to join those who doubt the existence of these fabled nomads – I can't believe anyone could survive in this parched wilderness – we stumble across a fire, embers still slightly smouldering. We press on for another ten minutes and then I hear a soft cough somewhere to my right. Naya holds up his hand for us to stop – there is somebody there. He goes to investigate, then beckons us forward.

Sitting on the forest floor in a small clearing is a family of four who look like they've been plucked straight from the pages of an illustrated school book about ancient mankind. A loincloth-clad mother and father and their two bright-eyed, cherubic daughters, who can be no more than one and three, stare wide-eyed back at us. The father acknowledges our presence with a genteel nod. Naya speaks softly to him in a Malagasy dialect. He wants to know where we're from but our attempts to explain England and the plane that flew us here are futile: "It's like a large bird that carries people through the sky" is met with blank looks and a bemused "We have never seen one."

The Mikea have no concept of life beyond this forest. They haven't even been to the sea, which is a mere five kilometres away. I imagine not knowing about Brexit and global warming and rush hour, but also not knowing about a really good book, the smell of fresh laundry, summer holidays. This level of disconnect is an entirely different playing field to the villagers we met the previous night – these people are some of the most secluded in the world. I wonder what thoughts enter their mind when they wake up, what they're looking forward to, if they're happy. Then I ask the same of myself.

In an era of "over tourism" I spend a great deal of time searching for "authentic" travel experiences – the word causes alarm bells to ring as it usually implies anything but. Madagascar wore away at my calcified shell of scepticism in a way that I could never have foreseen, proving that it is still possible to experience the untouched – but I wonder how long it will be before the Mikea know the deafening roar of aeroplanes all too well.

THE LOWDOWN

The ten-night Baobabs, Beaches & Bushtracks expedition with Natural World Safaris costs from £4,330 per person sharing and includes a private guide and vehicle, breakfast and dinner, internal flights and all activities

naturalworldsafaris.com

WHAT TO PACK
Madagascar

Photographer: MITCH PAYNE
Stylist: TONA STELL

1. Dr Roebuck's Daintree AHA Brightening Mask *£25,* **2. Elemental Herbology** Facial Detox Purifying Face Mask *£29,*
3. Bec & Bridge Tropical Fever Top in Yellow *£71,* **4. Masscob** Keira Shirt *£320,* **5. Tibi** Triacetate Beatle Pant in Pink
Haze *£415,* **6. Sunday Riley** CEO C+ E antiOXIDANT Protect + Repair Moisturiser *£60,* **7. Aesop** Rind Concentrate
Body Balm *£25*

8. **Marysia** Palm Springs Tie-Front Bikini Set £330, 9. **Birkenstock** Arizona Wool Felt in Double Face Orange £70,
10. **Saskia Diez x Viu** OH Limited Sunglasses in Sunshine Shiny £175, 11. **Smythson** Panama Large Zip Purse in Pink
£295, 12. **Nuxe** Huile Prodigieuse Multi-Purpose Dry Oil £29, 13. **Byredo** Suede Fragranced Soap £27, 14. **Fern Fans**
Plain Fan in Medium Yellow £55

Gin and Crocodiles

Skinny-dipping, stargazing and dancing in a sandstorm in the lesser-explored African nation of **Malawi**

———

Words by **ANNA HART**
Photos by **NATHAN LUNDA**

"There's no way I'll swim in Lake Malawi if there are crocodiles and parasites in there, and I'm not touching Malawi Gin," I pronounce confidently. My brother, Peter, had visited Malawi a couple of years ago while working at a hospital in neighbouring Zambia and was giving me the lowdown on the lake, Africa's third largest and populated with parasites and crocodiles. The gin, sold in sachets like cheap conditioner, sounded even more lethal.

A mere 24 hours later I'm skinny-dipping in the aforementioned lake with 15 strangers, tanked up on MG&Ts, as Malawians call their gin and tonics. Sure, I'll have a killer hangover, and yes, I'll have to pop a pill as a safeguard against parasites. But adventure is all about doing things that you never thought you would. Malawi – with a little bit of help from the 43-per-cent-proof gin – pushes me into an adventurous mindset at warp speed.

This was the first night of my ten-day group trip with Faraway, a brand-new and emphatically next-generation tour operator. Wife-and-husband team Helen and Al Robshaw fell in love with Malawi a few years ago and decided to build their dream itinerary around the Lake of Stars Festival, which has been taking place on the shores of Lake Malawi since 2004. Group travel can be a gamble and I pride myself on being an independent traveller. However, the thing about adventure is that it balances on a knife edge – too much and your journey slides into danger or discomfort, an ordeal rather than a thrill.

Malawi enjoys a reputation as a friendly, relaxed, and compact African nation but compared to neighbouring Mozambique, the tourism infrastructure is much less robust – the roads are less well-trodden and public transport is still a bit of an enigma. What small independent group ►►

DOMWE ISLAND

MUMBO ISLAND

operators like Faraway hope to do is open up new destinations like Malawi to solo travellers by removing the elements of risk and friction, leaving nothing but distilled discovery.

On our first morning we kayak from Cape Maclear (on the southern shore of Lake Malawi and a four-hour drive from Lilongwe, the capital city) to Domwe Island, a paddle of just over an hour. Apart from a handful of chefs and guides working with Kayak Africa, which owns Domwe and the nearby Mumbo Island, we have the entire island to ourselves. This knowledge fills us with an anarchic, castaway spirit, which explains the afternoon gin drinking, the dancing around the fire to Fela Kuti and the skinny-dipping by moonlight.

Malawi Gin has been distilled from sugar cane since the 1960s, perhaps a legacy from the Scottish missionaries – the first to enter the country was David Livingstone in 1859. MG&Ts might not protect us from bilharzia parasites or stray crocodiles (to be fair, they're a rare sight in the southern waters of the lake), but they certainly protect us from the fear of both. Before I left my brother had smiled at my confident assertions that I'd not set foot in the lake and gently murmured, "It's pretty tempting, Anna." He wasn't wrong. Carved out of the landscape by the Great Rift Valley, the colossal Lake Malawi looks like the sea, fringed with beaches and rocky islands. As soon as I see it, it seems perverse not to jump in.

For many years Malawi was dominated by its self-appointed "life president" Hastings Kamuzu Banda, who notoriously banned a Simon and Garfunkel song because the lyrics – "Cecilia, you're breaking my heart" – coincided with an emotional ruck happening with his long-term mistress and "official hostess of Malawi", Cecilia Tamanda Kadzamira. As you can imagine, Banda's other decisions weren't as absurdly amusing – political opponents and dissenting journalists were ruthlessly quashed until Banda's defeat in Malawi's first multi-party elections in 1994. Despite the prevailing poverty – Malawi has a primarily rural ▶▶

> 66 The colossal Lake Malawi looks like the sea, fringed with beaches and rocky islands"

and agricultural economy and remains heavily aid-dependent – this is a friendly, upbeat and welcoming nation and tourism is a fledgling industry most Malawians are keen to foster.

As we load up our kayaks the next morning to paddle across the shimmering waters to Mumbo Island, Malawi's potential as a tourist destination seems as vast as the lake. Yet tourism contributed just 4.5 per cent to the national GDP according to the most recent figures, compared to neighbouring Tanzania's 17.5 per cent. Responsible tourism isn't just about choosing sustainable hotels or stressing about your carbon footprint – it's also about thinking about where you spend your dollar and about redistributing it more fairly across the globe, ideally in places that can benefit from an additional source of income.

Mumbo Island takes the luxury up a notch from Domwe, where we had slept in tents on the beach. Mumbo is pricier, at £150 per person including food and bucketloads of gin, but the clifftop bungalows are among the most romantic I've ever set my bare foot in – the stuff that honeymoons are made of.

From the islands we jump in the bus and travel four hours south to the mountainous Zomba Plateau. Zomba Forest Lodge is run by Petal and Tom, who worked in events and hospitality in England for years before returning to Petal's homeland and adopting a 1920s bungalow, nurturing 20 acres of rainforest in a gully and helping to put this often-overlooked area on the map.

Tom and Petal are heavily involved in the anti-deforestation movement – forest fires are a regular occurrence and as we hike in Liwonde National Park we see swathes of supposedly protected forest razed to the ground. "Malawi suffers from the fastest rate of deforestation in Sub-Saharan Africa and right now, 95 per cent of the population still relies on firewood for both cooking and heating," Petal explains to me. They sponsor a local football team in Zomba, whose players also do double duty as volunteer firefighters in the case of a raging forest blaze.

Next we return to the lake, this time to Kumbali Lake Retreat in Salima, a short boat or bus ride along the beach from the site of the Lake of Stars Festival. 2018 marks 15 years since it was set up by Will Jameson, a British music lover who volunteered with the Wildlife Society in Malawi in 1998 and eventually returned in 2003 to encourage international tourism. Today it's one of the best-known African festivals on the global circuit, with African and international artists playing to a mixed crowd of locals and festival-lovers from the world over. After catching an acoustic set by Malawian superstar Lazarus and hip-hop by Lady Pace, we watch Major Lazer take to the main stage in the midst of a sandstorm. There's a fashion show, a pop-up roller disco and performance poetry by Hollie McNish and Michael Pederson. It's a triumph, although having danced through a sandstorm I'll never complain about a muddy British festival again.

After washing the grit out of our ears we make our way to Majete Wildlife Reserve. Mkulumadzi Lodge is a cluster of eight stylish chalets overlooking a river where elephants and hippos roam. Majete is a Big Five park without the hefty price tags or the roar of packed Land Rovers. It's here that I say goodbye to Malawi the best way I know how – by spending the night with it under the stars on a raised deck or "sky bed". When the last thing you see at night is the vastness of the universe, you can't carry any petty concerns or anxieties into your dreams with you. I wake up gently to a reddening sky, feeling like the luckiest – and also the only – person on the planet. Adventure does this to you. And Malawi certainly knows how to serve up an adventure.

THE LOWDOWN

The ten-day Malawi trip with Faraway starts from £2,800 at an early bird rate and not including flights

wearefaraway.com

> 66 Having danced through a sandstorm I'll never complain about a muddy British festival again"

LAKE OF STARS

MKULUMADZI LODGE

MAJETE WILDLIFE RESERVE

Above and Beyond

The Big Five are flourishing in an immersive conservation experience deep in South Africa's **KwaZulu-Natal** province

———

Words and photos by
LIZ SEABROOK

After close to 24 hours of travelling, including a 90-minute drive from Johannesburg, I'm jolted awake as our car passes through the security gate of Phinda Private Game Reserve. In spite of my weary state, my eyes widen as I silently stare out of the window, wondering what animals might be roaming the 17,000 hectares that lie beyond.

I've been told to expect encounters with the local community as well as animals during my time at KwaZulu-Natal province's first Big Five game reserve. Established in 1991, Phinda is the founding reserve of the operator andBeyond and the lessons learned here through rewilding the land, reintroducing vulnerable species and engaging with surrounding communities have shaped the company into a pioneering force in ecotourism.

I arrive at the beautiful Phinda Homestead where I'm greeted by host William de Jager and his right-hand man Mandla Mnguni with hot towels and a tray of lime and ginger drinks. Newly rebuilt following a fire in 2016, the lodge's four rooms are structured around a covered terrace, accented with a mixture of traditional crafts and modern South African art, and face out onto a watering hole. "The elephants aren't here today," laughs William, explaining that during the build the watering hole had to be widened to stop the creatures' trunks from dipping into the swimming pool. I can't help but secretly feel a little disappointed.

However, this sensation quickly dissipates as I'm shown to my room. Endless windows, natural wood and burnt-orange furnishings blend seamlessly into the natural surroundings – I'm tempted to have a lie-down, but instead find myself being whisked back out to meet the Homestead's private ranger, Clive Cowie, and tracker, Muzi Mtshali. Sitting shotgun at the front of the vehicle, Muzi's sharp eyes scour the undergrowth, trees and thickets for any movement. Nearly all of the trackers working on the reserve – Muzi included – come from the local community and many hone their skills from working on the family farm, venturing out into the bush to find cattle or goats gone rogue.

As we cruise along a bumpy, tree-lined track the radio on the dash crackles with updates of sightings from other rangers across the reserves. Something piques Clive's interest and he spins around, blue eyes glittering with excitement. There's a lion sighting on the plains and it's mating season. Picking up speed, we emerge onto open grassland where, just a few metres in front of the car, a lion and lioness are sitting. Clive kills the engine, allowing Muzi to clamber down off the bonnet into the safety of the front passenger seat. The scenario starts with the lion climbing on top of the lioness and ends with her snapping at him, and I giggle at the parallels between humankind and the animal kingdom. Clive turns, kneeling up on his seat like an excited schoolboy, "That's a really rare thing to see, and you've seen it on your first drive!" ▶

PHINDA HOMESTEAD

A cacophony of croaks provides the soundtrack for our dinner that evening, a delicious three-course meal whipped up by the talented resident chef Lucky. Our conversation reveals Mandla's connection to Phinda runs deeper than a mere job – his father was the first chef at the reserve when it was founded in 1991. Each day he would climb a tree outside the lodge and announce the menu. When he got too old, he hobbled onto a bench. One of 15 siblings, today Mandla and his brother are the two who have decided to carry on their father's legacy.

I'm up at 5.45am the next day for another drive. The early morning mist lifts to reveal something moving cautiously in the long grass that turns out to be a mother cheetah and her cubs. One of the first animals to be reintroduced to Phinda in 1991, cheetah are listed as vulnerable on the International Union for Conservation of Nature Red List of Threatened Species, chiefly due to loss of habitat. The attentive mother suckles and cleans her young, her ears pricked to scan for danger – or perhaps dinner. Suddenly, she's on her feet. Slowly she crouches before setting off in hot pursuit of a scrub hare. Not long after chasing her prey into a thicket she emerges triumphant, the hare hanging limp in her jaws. Again, Clive is up in his seat. "Cheetahs are usually unsuccessful hunters, and you've seen a kill!" He shakes his head, presumably wondering how he will be able to top this.

After a hearty breakfast of pancakes, huevos rancheros and William's favourite health shot, Bheki Ntuli from the Africa Foundation – andBeyond's sister charity focusing on community relations – drives us to a local school. Out of the office strides a beaming Mrs Zikhali. She is the sort of woman you want to see leading generations of children – fierce, strong and full of heart. She tells us how at just 15 she fled Johannesburg to avoid being traded for 11 cows as part of a dowry to be a man's fifth wife. By 1998, she was single-handedly running and teaching a school of 60 pupils ten kilometres from her home and only accessible by boat via a fast-flowing river. Together with the community, Mrs Zikhali decided to move the school to its current site beneath two trees with twisted roots for seats – one her office, the other her classroom. She shares her account of the time an andBeyond guest visited the school while the children were on a break. When the children returned, she was greeted by a young student with a face of thunder tugging on her sleeve. "Mrs Zikhali, you've made a terrible mistake." The child then turned to point at the guest's car, "He's parked in our classroom!" This guest went on to donate over 100,000 rand to the school.

Today, thanks largely to Mrs Zikhali's passion and perseverance, the school educates some 900 students with a teaching staff of 36. She has also adopted five children from the school – one is ▶▶

MRS ZIKHALI

NYATHI ANTI-POACHING UNIT

now a doctor, one an electrician and another a pharmacist, while the other two are still studying. My eyes prick with admiration to stand alongside this wonderful woman. Elsewhere in the community a number of other schools have been built thanks to money raised by andBeyond and the Africa Foundation, including a facility specialising in caring for children with special needs, two clinics, a bakery and a space for local craftswomen to sell their wares. Local builders are used wherever possible and those with more experience are helped to set up their own companies.

Back on another early game drive it seems that all the grazing animals have come to meet us – first zebra, then a giraffe, then a whole herd of buffalo. Our 4x4 splashes through the shallows of a watering hole as a hippo yawns in the distance. Then, there they are – a crash of nine white rhinos munching away. Rhino poaching is at an all-time high in South Africa, with more being killed each year than are born. In 2016 andBeyond took the difficult decision to dehorn its rhinos – a process akin to cutting a fingernail that must be repeated every 18 to 24 months and which has been shown to cause no behavioural changes in the

animals. Without its horn a rhino is of no interest to poachers, but South Africa remains an unsafe place for these creatures and the cost of security is near crippling in spite of an increase in donations. Consequently andBeyond has partnered with fellow operator Great Plains Conservation on the Rhinos without Borders initiative, in which 87 rhinos to date have been relocated to safer pastures in neighbouring Botswana. Guests of the reserve can opt to take part in the process of tagging the rhinos, resulting in an immersive experience that often sees them donating large sums to support andBeyond's conservation efforts. After the joy of being surrounded by so many of Africa's iconic animals seeing the rhinos is sobering, particularly in the knowledge that they are only here thanks to the hard work of a handful of individuals.

That afternoon I meet Dale Wepener, who heads up the habitat team, alongside Barend Lottering of the Nyathi Anti-Poaching Unit. The APU plays a vital role not only in the protection of the reserve but also within the community, offering stable employment and educating people in the importance of caring for wildlife. As we talk Barend makes some clicking sounds into

his walkie-talkie. Moments later six men in camouflage carrying assorted semi-automatic rifles and machetes emerge from the trees around us. These are Phinda's guardians, all hailing from the local Zulu communities. Some have been part of the unit for more than a decade, some joined so that their children could grow up in a world with the wildlife they have been able to experience, and others are former poachers turned good. Dale and another member of the habitat team head off into the bush and soon after the APU go in after them, marking any suspicious-looking footprints in the grass and sand. When they catch poachers they need to be able to stand up in court to deliver evidence, plaster-of-Paris footprints included.

The next day we're joined on our final drive by Craig Sholto-Douglas, an environmental researcher with andBeyond, who brings along the telemetry kit used to track some of the collared elephants. Craig picks up a strong signal which leads us to a nearby watering hole, where four herds of elephants are splashing around in the rain. They start dunking each other, swishing their trunks and trumpeting away, as if to mock the dark clouds gathered overhead. These animals are majestic, enormous beasts, but in this moment they just seem like big kids.

As I wait to disembark from a small airstrip I spot three giraffes munching from some trees, creating a final postcard-perfect image. As I wave goodbye to Clive and Muzi, I'm overwhelmed by a deep sense of connection to this miraculous place and the animals and people who live here. This is, I realise, the andBeyond model in action – I'm a guest leaving, wanting to do more.

THE LOWDOWN

andBeyond Phinda Homestead from £4,162 per villa per night. This includes a private vehicle, all food and beverages, laundry, safari activities and return transfers to the lodge airstrip

andbeyond.com

Might and Magic

Navigating Indonesia's remote **Banda Islands**
in the slipstream of spice-greedy colonialists
reveals a land that time forgot

―――

Words by **IMOGEN LEPERE**
Photos by **BILLY BOLTON**

With the right wind you'll smell the Banda Islands before you see them. Also known as the Spice Islands, this archipelago of ten volcanic eruptions in the remote backwaters of the East Indies is so small that modern-day cartographers often overlook it. Yet in the 17th century, Portugal, Britain and Holland fought over them bitterly, for their mineral-rich soil nurtures a fragrant secret. They were the only place in the world where nutmegs grew, a spice once worth more than gold because of its exotic, romantic flavour and the fact that it was rumoured to cure the plague. In those days money quite literally grew on trees for those prepared to overcome shipwrecks, warring tribes and tropical diseases to claim the spice.

A phinisi (a traditional wooden vessel) named Tiger Blue is carrying me in the wake of explorers such as Sir Francis Drake, Ferdinand Magellan and countless others through the Maluku region to the Banda Islands. We're travelling 800 nautical miles over 11 days through the famously fierce Banda Sea from Maumere to Ambon, diving with hammerhead sharks, meeting local tribes and spotting sperm whales along the way. With just two other guests on board and a ten-strong crew of sea dogs and dive specialists, it doesn't get much more exclusive than this. A habitual landlubber, it's my first experience of living on a boat and I airily dismiss the captain's offer of a seasickness pill. How rough can the seas really be?

One of our first nights at sea answers my question. For hours I lurk in my cabin as three-metre waves pummel the ship from all sides. It bucks like a stallion and I can't help but think of the earthquake and tsunami that tragically struck Sulawesi the night before our trip, despite the fact we are more than 1,000km away. The crew are unfazed, shimmying up ladders made lethally slippery by the sea's spray as easily as a flight of stairs, while the chef coolly whips up a delicious spread of Indonesian dishes. We've been told that the best protection against seasickness is a full stomach, so I set to with gusto. Throughout our journey this beaming man cooks up everything from Lebanese mezze to crème brûlée that would put any Parisian bistro to shame in a kitchen smaller than a double bed.

The soft, peachy glow of sunrise filtering through the porthole wakes us gently. We've dropped anchor in the natural harbour of Kalabahi on Alors Island, a moon of water so enclosed it's as calm as a lake. The watery hills and lurching valleys of the night before seem but a distant dream. On the shore the outline of a mosque rises through the morning mist and the sound of the imam calling the people to prayer echoes across the glassy water. The silvery gleam of flying fish catches my eye and I look down. Local fishermen in wooden canoes are silently circling the boat, their faces shadows beneath wide-brimmed hats. A thin spire of smoke emerges from the dense forest that cloaks the hillside. It feels as if anything could happen.   ▶▶

A bumpy drive into the mountains and we are face-to-face with a group of elders from the Abui tribe, their teeth crimson with betel-nut juice. "They were headhunters until quite recently. Warlike peoples. Now their only chance to practise their traditions is when visitors come to the village," our guide Ahmed, a local tribesman himself, tells us. "See the little ones?" He gestures to several children watching the elders in awe. "This is how they learn the ways of their people. It protects their customs for the next generation and gives them the money to keep living in their ancestral homes."

The village feels as if it fell asleep several centuries ago and woke to find its thatched houses on stilts, the tribesmen's fierce swords and jangle of the women's heavy ankle rings severely at odds with the "new" world they find themselves in. It's a daily battle to prevent their culture from being eroded by the nearby town that is slowly spreading towards them. "It's mostly the very old and children who are here. The ocean takes the middle-aged to work on fishing boats. Those who are left are very worried about the tribe's future," Ahmed continues. Looking around I see a wily chief in a feathered headdress pulling on a Marlboro Red. When one of the women reaches into the folds of her ikat (a handwoven cloth that's unique to the region), pulls out a phone and asks for a selfie, the uneasy conflict between past and present is evident.

The region's natural wonders are also swimming hard against the tide of modernity and the consumerist culture that's so entwined with it. Once we pause in an inky channel because the crew have heard there might be dugongs (a manatee-like mammal) there. On a sand bar hundreds of miles from civilisation two shadowy figures appear and the ship's radio crackles. The local tribe wants to know our intentions. In exchange for a bag of rice and some fuel they're happy to let us look for the dugong Mawar ("Roses" in their language), but warn us not to swim with him. A commercial fishing boat killed his mate and he's so lonely there's a chance he may drag any living thing down to the depths for company. We spend a few minutes quietly floating in the bay until Mawar emerges of his own accord. Dugongs are often curious and he's keen to investigate. After a few minutes of swimming under and around us, he clutches the rubber side of the dinghy tightly in his flippers and looks at us with strangely human eyes. The boat is roughly seven feet long, the same size as him, and I have the uncomfortable suspicion it reminds him of his mate.

At Serua Island, where jets of warm air from a volcano nourish a thriving coral reef, we snorkel and dive. This volcanic spire is so steep that even the island's 100 residents have never been able to penetrate the thick jungle on its upper slopes and the mysterious creatures that live there may never be seen. Below water the reef is a whirligig of surreal corals – pink frills like a ballerina's tutu, bulging brains and upright antlers with flashes of electric blue darting between them, while the ominous shape of hammerhead sharks loom in the shadows of the drop. ▶▶

A flash of yellow in a coral cave catches my eye – a butterfly or parrot fish, perhaps? Despite the fact that we're a 19-hour sail in any direction from another island it turns out to be an empty shampoo bottle, discarded in a moment and destined to pollute this reef for the foreseeable future. As I reach to pick it up a pair of clownfish swim out and nudge my hand away from their unusual home, while a translucent seahorse shyly curls itself around the neck of the bottle. It's a powerful reminder about the lasting impacts of single-use plastic. Tiger Blue tackles this problem head on, supplying us with reusable water bottles and eco-friendly toiletries that don't pollute the incredible seascapes that make our adventure possible.

As we sail on, the water becomes as blue as a peacock's tail. The boat's movements are more like the gentle rise and fall of a carousel pony than the bucking stallion of the nights before. Suddenly a dolphin leaps out of our bow wave, its back arching gleefully. The crew quickly lower the dinghy and as we zoom out the pod surrounds us, leaping and changing direction with our boat until it feels like we're actually part of it. Back on Tiger Blue I turn on my phone to Google what species they were. There's no signal and I find I'm content lying on the bow in the sun, feeling the spray on my skin and listening to the dolphins whistle.

Crossing the Banda Sea, the swell picks up again and the boat groans and creaks like an arthritis sufferer getting out of bed on a winter's morning. We shelter in our cabin watching the waves crash over the porthole. As night falls the sea calms a little and we climb to the top deck, where the captain scans the empty horizon. Dark ocean bleeds into sky and the creamy smudge of the Milky Way is reflected on the water. It feels like we're sailing through the stars.

When we finally reach the Banda Islands it seems as if we did in fact sail into another galaxy. A winding entrance between slopes cloaked in virgin jungle leads to an inland bay between Neira and the Api volcano, which occasionally belches evil-smelling smoke. Memories of the islands' pivotal role in history are everywhere. A Dutch fort looms above the jumble of colourful cottages that make up Neira town, while the waterfront is lined with once-grand colonial mansions, many with broken chandeliers and period furniture still languishing in their dusty rooms. On the side of the road a gentle street vendor asks if I'd like to buy any of the Dutch coins and rusty ship's parts that he digs up frequently in the harbour. The local houses are rainbow-coloured and bustling with life. Chickens peck among burning nutmeg shells in the yards – a local trick to ward off mosquitoes – while children jump in and out of the water, watched over by elderly men in longboats. As we pass by they smile and wave. Given that Indonesia's independence was only finally gained as recently as 1945, their friendliness seems generous. ▶ ▶

Plants thrive on the volcanic soil. In the shade of an overgrown plantation our guide plucks the fruit of the nutmeg tree, split open just enough to reveal the nut in its mesh of dragon's-blood-red mace, and in the next movement peels back a strip of cinnamon bark. The sun-wizened nenek (grandma) who now owns the plantation shyly offers us cups of cinnamon and mace tea alongside crumbly sponge cake coated in nutmeg jam. One bite and we can see why people were once prepared to die for its heady, mystical taste. If the British hadn't plundered several hundred nutmeg seedlings from these fragrant gardens in the early 1800s and created their own plantations in Singapore and Ceylon, it's easy to imagine that the Banda Islands would be as highly contested now as they ever were.

As we prepare to leave the bay a kora-kora boat paddled by 34 of Neira's strongest men floats alongside us. They escort Tiger Blue out of their waters with a masculine display of synchronised rowing and chanting that demonstrates that this beautiful place has always been theirs, whatever the colonists may have believed.

Our journey continues past the island of Run. A sleepy speck just two miles long, it is so thick with nutmeg groves that the Dutch gave the British the island of Manhattan in exchange for it and considered this an excellent deal. We devour tuna sashimi that was caught just hours before and watch as the island's white sands and emerald jungles slide by. I vaguely think about taking a picture before realising I have no idea where my phone is. On a wooden sailing boat somewhere between the swells of the Banda Sea and fragrant shores of the Spice Islands, it seems that I have found something even more precious than nutmeg: the peace that comes from surrendering to the might and magic of the ocean.

THE LOWDOWN

Ampersand Travel offers 11 nights on Tiger Blue from £9,620 per person, based on two people sharing a cabin and including transfers, domestic and international flights

ampersandtravel.com

An earthquake and tsunami hit Central Sulawesi in September 2018, with more than 2,000 people reportedly killed and 83,000 displaced. Unicef has launched a public appeal to help provide humanitarian assistance in the region. To find out more and donate, visit Unicef Next Generation London's Indonesia appeal

justgiving.com/fundraising/nextgenforindonesia

The Shape of Water

Experiencing the immense underwater world through the eyes of the champion freediver, marine conservationist and founder of I AM WATER

Words by **HANLI PRINSLOO**
Photos by **PETER MARSHALL**

Freediving (diving without breathing equipment) is as much a mental as a physical sport. For over ten years I've been exploring the limits of both my body and mind in the water. My fascination with the human body's mammalian dive response has kept me committed to an activity most people have never heard of, while those who have think we're all crazy adrenalin seekers. Nothing could be further from the truth.

I AM WATER was founded on the overwhelming connection I feel with nature and specifically with the ocean when I freedive, and the belief that this connection should be accessible to everyone. In my home country of South Africa our conservation foundation works with thousands of students in schools in under-served communities, who despite being within walking distance of the beach have never had a real ocean experience.

Our teams of coaches share yoga and mindfulness practices, lead rock-pool explorations, give marine ecosystem education and, of course, take the children snorkelling, allowing them to safely see the world beneath the waves – the kelp forests full of light and life, the pink and purple urchins, the bright-orange starfish, and the myriad octopi, penguins, seals and otters. Meanwhile, our travel arm puts people face-to-face with these creatures in order to fund our conservation work and inspire them to protect the ocean in their own lives in whatever small (or large) way that they can. These are some of the moments that have lingered with me on my journey to understanding the power and potential of those lesser-explored, submerged parts of our planet. ▶ ▶

DOLPHINS
Mozambique,
November 2007

———

I was going to set the rope a little deeper that day.

I'd been teaching freediving for weeks without doing any deep dives of my own and I was getting nervous. The world championships were only six weeks away and I was aiming for another African record – maybe even a world record. We leave the beach early before the wind picks up and before breakfast – it's better to hold your breath on an empty stomach, they say. Summertime in Mozambique sees the sun rise before six and it glows on the horizon as we push the boat through the waves. "We need to go further out to find you more depth," the skipper shouts over his shoulder. I nod and close my eyes, deepening my breath to slow my heart rate and oxygenate my blood.

As the sun climbs higher above us and the green of the coastline grows blurry in the distance, the skipper suddenly slows down. "Dolphins! Hundreds of spinners!" he cries as the ocean erupts with lithe, slate-grey bodies, effortlessly gliding through the water before launching, spinning up into the air like a tornado of mercury twirling into the sky. I grab my mask and pull on my monofin, my feet together like a mermaid's tail. The skipper shakes his head: "No use Han – these spinners aren't interested in humans. They'll just swim away if we stop the boat."

My heart is hammering in my chest, deep breathing and heart-rate control out of the window as my every fibre longs to join the dance. I've never swum

> **"** I am in a whirlpool of curious dolphins that click, whistle and crackle around me**"**

with dolphins before. "Please," I beg, "just let me jump in." I get an impatient shrug of the shoulders but he cuts the motors and I go. One deep breath, a few kicks of my fin and I'm with them. Large dark eyes move closer as I kick further down. "They're not leaving," I think as more and more dolphins join the swirling mass of bodies around me.

I try to move just like them, all my years of swimming up and down a rope, lengths along the black line at the bottom of the swimming pool suddenly paying off. I am part of the pod. I am in a whirlpool of curious dolphins that click, whistle and crackle around me, talking to each other and scanning me up and down: "Who is this pale, soft mammal who moves like us?" We reach the sandy bottom in a tangle of fins and flukes and I look up at the silhouettes layered above me, adults and babies in twos and threes, whole squadrons of perfectly synchronised bodies. They are so close I could touch them. They start circling me as we slowly swim up towards the surface, their intelligent eyes watching me. I look back and know that nothing could possibly be the same again.

This life, this freedom, this sentience – it exists out here, just below the surface. As I break through I know I'll do anything to ensure that these creatures get to retain this wild joy – that I'll never want to do anything else other than protect their world. I never did break that world record – there are too many oceans to explore, underwater friendships to forge and conservation efforts to launch. ▸▸

JACKFISH
Mexico,
November 2017

———

Along the Baja coastline the red sand meets the blue ocean and the iconic cacti stand watch as we shun the land and explore the sea. Jacques Cousteau once called the Sea of Cortez the "world's aquarium" and thanks to the great efforts of a local community of fishermen turned divers, this is still true today. As we travel out to sea with our expert skipper David, the son of Mario, who dedicated his life to convincing his town to stop fishing, he stops the boat. "Here," he says, "I can smell them." We look at each other disbelievingly but put on masks and fins and slide into a silver world.

Larger than a basketball field and stretching deeper than 20m, the giant school of jackfish swirl below us. I take a big breath and dive down as stealthily

as I can. If disturbed the giant school acts as one spirit and splinters away. However, as I swim very slowly towards them, one languid kick at a time, the school opens before me and I'm swallowed into the glowing ball of fish.

At over a foot long, they are not small. Slowly I start seeing individuals. Eyes and fins and tails. As I dive deeper down they close above me and I'm surrounded, immersed in a spectacle that has become so very rare – an ocean full of life, a magical place where we are completely outnumbered. ▶ ▶

"Wait, can you spell that for me?" is the first thing I say when my sailor friend Joe first tells me about the tiny limestone rock cast away in the middle of the South Pacific. With only two flights a week from Auckland, this autonomous nation is hardly known outside of New Zealand. I zoom out on the map until eventually Samoa, Fiji and Tonga pop up. This small green dot feels very far from everything – except humpback whales, that is.

Every year the whales travel from Antarctica up to the South Pacific to give birth, mate and prepare their young for the long journey back at the season's end. Niue is not a hotspot like neighbouring Tonga – the whales pass through for just a few days at a time, not the weeks and months they spend in the shallow lagoons of other islands. This is exactly why we like it. The proud Niueans have carefully observed their visitors and made decisions based on the wellbeing of all, with very few permits for whale swim operators and a "no diving down" policy to ensure the whales are never put under pressure from either boats or people.

After quietly observing three whales and confirming the right conditions for a swim we slip into the water. Looking down I see their enormous blue-grey backs resting just ten metres below us and feast my eyes on their iconic knobbly heads and ludicrously long pectoral fins. Five, ten, 15 minutes pass as we wait. The whales have been watching us as we have been watching them – it is completely their choice if they want to investigate. In slow motion they start coming up, floating vertically like giant, fat angels. The first one decides to emerge right beside us and we stare transfixed at her white belly. She exhales loudly.

Suddenly I glance behind us and see a second whale swimming right towards us, turning slightly to observe us before surfacing beside me. Staring into that large, wrinkled eye I see her looking back at me. What does she see? For the half hour we are in the water we don't say a word. The whales hang around, accepting our presence. Then as one they take a last breath and dive. Bereft, we watch them disappear into the blue.

HUMPBACK WHALES
Niue,
September 2018
—

WHALE SHARKS
Madagascar,
October 2018

Working with a local researcher and a highly reputable operator we spend hours at sea exploring this wild pocket of the Indian Ocean. In one week we see over ten individual whale sharks, super pods of spinner dolphins, quietly feeding turtles and squadrons of mobula rays. The white beaches are scattered with cowrie shells, gigantic mango trees drip with fruit and groves of sweet-smelling ylang ylang plantations fringe the bays.

This wild island is already well-known for its staggering terrestrial biodiversity, but the small island of Nosy Be just off its northwestern tip is making a claim as a home for the greatest of all fish – the whale shark. In most places around the world where whale sharks congregate it is to feed, and the water is typically murky from all the plankton. In the Philippines they are fed by local fishermen who want to keep them in the area for tourism, which has devastating effects on their wellbeing, while in other places tourism is so poorly regulated that there are often over 300 boats in the water

offering the opportunity to swim with the sharks. In short, to have the privilege of swimming alongside a majestic whale shark without it being to the detriment of the animal is not as easy as it looks on Instagram.

In the water, I gaze down at the broad back of a whale shark. It's like staring up at the Milky Way – bright pinpricks of white on a midnight-blue back, each creature unique. The Malagasy name for whale shark is "marokintana", meaning many stars. She is a constellation fingerprint.

THE LOWDOWN

I AM Water Ocean Travel expeditions run throughout the year, with prices differing depending on destination

iamwateroceantravel.com

Pastures New

Herding reindeer with Norway's Sami people
for the annual migration from **Sørøya** island

—

Words and photos by
ARON KLEIN

Five flights, one snowstorm and an airport that consists of four chairs and not much else later from stepping out of my front door, I arrive in the snow-capped region of Hasvik on the Norwegian island of Sørøya. Undoubtedly you've never heard of it, unless you're an overly keen fisherman who's kept an eye on the exact locations of recent deep-sea fishing world records.

However, I'm not here for the fish. I'm here because this remote island, deep in the Arctic Circle and at the northernmost tip of Norway, is the traditional summer home of the Sami people. For thousands of years these indigenous people have co-existed with reindeer herders (also known as boazovázzi) and each year they make the pilgrimage to follow thousands of deer from their lush summer pastures on the island to the wintering grounds on the mainland's tundra. With the creatures outnumbering humans by a ratio of six to one, this is no easy task – particularly as during the summer grazing season the deer will have spread across the island's unforgiving mountainous terrain. Around 40 Sami must club together to corral them using modern luxuries such as boats, motorbikes, ATVs and even a helicopter to locate the stragglers. The whole process can take up to a month.

I join the tribe at the end of September just as the winter migration preparations are beginning and am greeted by Nils Sara, the father of the Sami family with whom I'll be staying. We've been introduced by Visit Natives, a travel agency dedicated to supporting the herders' lifestyle through small-scale tourism and homestays with local families. Founder Anniina Sandberg was inspired to protect the indigenous culture of her homeland after spending nine months living with a Maasai tribe in Tanzania. The majority of the money raised goes directly to Sami families in order that they may better be able to resist the financial pressure to move to the cities in search of alternative work, thus preserving the culture of herding for the next generation.

The importance of this mission is brought home to me when I meet Nils' ten-year-old son (and total badass) Hendrick, who having inherited calves from the age of two is now a seasoned veteran with his own lasso, knife and small herd. Unfortunately for me the herding process, due to begin on the day I arrive, has had to be postponed thanks to unseasonably bad weather – the warmer summers and unpredictable winters brought about by climate change are known to affect the herding patterns, although it's impossible to say for sure if this is the case here. Instead, I head out to the still-grassy and golden hills under Hendrick and Nils' guidance to watch them constructing the goahti, the traditional tepee-like structure that will be their home for the two months that the migration lasts.

As the evening draws in Nils shows me how to smoke reindeer meat over a low fire, which his family will enjoy with foraged berries, sweet flatbread and mountain-herb tea in a meal that almost has me questioning my vegetarianism. Sitting on a deerskin rug alongside them, it's a timeless scene and an opportunity to slow down before the real work begins. Before we sleep Nils takes me outside and explains how lucky he feels to live with the same great sense of purpose as his forefathers. It's only as we move further into the darkness that I realise the sky is dancing with green light. I've been so exhausted and focused on the prospect of reindeer that I'd completely forgotten I'm in the land of the Northern Lights.

The next two days are spent preparing for the arrival of the reindeer, with the whole family falling into their individual roles. Everything must be ready to go as the timing of the migration and route taken is up to the deer themselves – "We are just there as guides," Nils laughs. We set about organising rations and stretching out the lassos that have been stored for the summer. Hendrick suddenly tells me to run and before I know it, he has me tightly tangled up in his ropes. Before he releases me, he can't resist smugly pointing out that the deer have four legs and antlers to contend with, making me twice as difficult to catch – and yet I still miserably failed to get away.

Each member of the family wears the same colourful, hand-made clothes as their ancestors did, to which they will add reindeer furs when the temperature drops. No Gore-Tex jacket could compete in the depths of winter, they tell me. It's a necessary precaution – once the deer arrive to the corral, the families can be working for more than 24 hours at a time, sleeping on the mountain in long, gruelling days and nights that merge into a blur. It might seem like a tough life – but these are the Sami, and the desire to work alongside nature this way is in their blood.

THE LOWDOWN

The three-night Sami experience with Visit Natives in winter costs £1,740 and includes accommodation with a family in a cabin, traditional Sami food, transportation via snowmobile and warm winter outerwear

visitnatives.com

For more information about Sami culture and northern Norway go to *visitnorway.com*

Long Day's Journey into Night

A polar safari on the cusp of the seasons
in Norway's **Svalbard** archipelago

Words by OLIVIA SQUIRE
Photos by BENJAMIN HARDMAN

I skitter and stumble my way across the pebbly plain, trying to avoid stepping on the bursts of mustard-coloured moss that have somehow sprouted in this most inhospitable of places. Triangular peaks as rigid as the arms of a compass puncture an endlessly blank sky, while the gargantuan slopes of their elders yawn down to the blasted earth below. Acres of shale stretch out before me, broken only by fragments of whale bone and the brackish sea surging to my right. The sheer scale of it all means that time and distance both dissipate – as soon as I pause to catch my breath the mountains recede and loom all at once, a magic-eye pattern whirling against the wind. Mars would be too cheap an analogy for this sense of weightlessness, of being untethered from my very self. Purgatory might be better.

Svalbard is a land of both extremes and in-betweens. The archipelago is situated between 74° and 81° north, a thousand miles from the Norwegian mainland and at the very end of the earth. From April to August it is bleached in eternal daylight and from the close of October until February it plunges into perpetual darkness. Centuries of explorers, hunters and miners have variously tried (and sometimes failed) to conquer its soaring shores, and both blood and blubber mingle in their tales of dominion and disaster.

Yet there is nuance hidden between Svalbard's theatrical landscapes and legends. Humanity is a relatively recent intervention here and consequently there is no framework of culture, art or ancient history from which to hang my impressions. It is a place of passage rather than of permanence – it is literally forbidden by law to be born or to die here, as there are no hospitals or burial grounds – and its monochromatic vistas with their slate-grey seas, powdery mountains and smudges of cloud suggest a withholding, as well as perhaps an invitation. It's a place that can make or break you, and consequently an intoxicating challenge to the pioneer spirit.

The majority of travellers are drawn here for the winter season when the frozen fjords and whitewashed mountains transform the islands into a kind of Arctic theme park, giving intrepid adventurers the opportunity to slide across the horizon via dog sled, snowmobile or ski, or else embark on more northerly expeditions. When the snow melts away in the summer the most popular excursions are through the fjords by boat. At any time of year all will be hoping to spot Svalbard's most famous inhabitant, the polar bear, which outnumbers the human population at roughly 3,000 compared to 2,200. ▶ ▶

Our photographer Ben and I arrive at the balancing point between the seasons, just before the polar night tips over and the first snow begins to fall. We're greeted by an alarmingly matter-of-fact sign informing us that a polar bear and her two cubs have recently been spotted feasting on a whale carcass just outside of town, an early indication of how closely knotted the wild and the pragmatic are here. Driving into Longyearbyen, the only real settlement on Svalbard's Spitsbergen Island, the spindly remnants of mining structures lean drunkenly from the hillsides, haunted houses propped up on stilts, and the sweeping, zebra-striped mountains that are scratched into the sky give the impression of chalk wiped from a blackboard.

Our destination is the Basecamp Hotel, one of several Svalbard outposts run by the sustainable, low-impact tour operator Basecamp Explorer. In an effort to reflect the lifestyle of the early trappers (hunters) who settled here – albeit in a rather more comfortable way – its wooden corridors are littered with artefacts including lanterns, taxidermied birds, nautical maps, hessian coffee-bean sacks and glass cases filled with miniature bottles of cognac. I resist the temptation to hole up in my cosy cocoon of a room with one of the proffered mugs of hot chocolate and instead head into the chill to explore Basecamp's nearby Trapper's Station, home to its 90 huskies.

The practice of trapping, whereby hunters would live largely in isolation in the wilderness to gather and sell the pelts of Arctic foxes and polar bears, peaked in the early 1900s. Today there are only three trappers left on the archipelago, the hunting of polar bears is strictly forbidden and the dogs at the Trapper's Station are used for the purposes of sledding only. In homage to the islands' history the station has been designed with two replica cabins where guests can sleep over if they choose, alongside gruesome relics of the trapper lifestyle such as a seal post, where seal carcasses were strung up to escape the clutches of hungry polar bears, and a shotgun trap formerly used to "humanely" kill the bears. I'm more enchanted by the dozens of yelping dogs with curious names – Instagram and Twitter, Odin and Lyra, and Eminem, ever the outcast, in the middle – who leap up until their paws rest on my shoulders and their piercing blue eyes bore into mine. ▶ ▶

Upon our return to the hotel we're told there's a chance our scheduled boat excursion into the fjords the next day might have to be postponed due to choppy waters – a couple of unlucky travellers have been stranded at our next stop, Hotel Isfjord Radio, for almost a week. It's a reminder that we're completely beholden to the whims of nature, so to blunt the spectre of a thwarted trip we head out to explore Longyearbyen's surprisingly buzzy bars and restaurants. Stationen could be mistaken for any other hip Scandi dining spot were it not for the multiple "No Guns Allowed" signs and whale burger on the menu (I politely decline), and the bars at the Karlsberger Pub, Barentz Pub and Svalbar are testament to the fact that the inhabitants of Svalbard drink more alcohol per person than in any other region of Norway – a strategy for dealing with those infinitely long days and nights, no doubt.

The next morning it becomes apparent that we won't be needing to drown our sorrows just yet – the waters have stilled and we're given the go-ahead to proceed to Isfjord. After struggling into full-body, bright-orange, waterproof suits that give us the look of bloated convicts, we pile into our open RIB boat. As the engine gets going I shove some acid-yellow goggles over my bobble hat and the world tilts an acrid shade of Mountain Dew, just one more dose of unreality in this strange and confronting corner of the globe. We're taking the penultimate boat trip of the season and as such much of the wildlife has already departed, leaving us with the bare bones of a barren landscape not yet sugar-coated with snow. I try to avoid gulping mouthfuls of hair as we stream across the hard, pewter sheet of water into the biting wind.

An inestimable amount of time later we scramble up the dock at Isfjord Radio and are greeted with chipped mugs of gratifyingly warm mulled wine. Formerly a radio station built in 1933 to assist communications with the mainland, today this unassuming collection of buildings forms a boutique hotel. The station is still used by the coastguard and airport, as evidenced by the white satellite dish that towers over the sage-green main building. We gladly shed our tangerine shells and head inside to discover a palette of greys, greens and browns inspired by the light and colours outside, as well as remnants of the station's history in the form of old typewriters, cases of books and knotted bundles of cables hanging from the walls. ▶▶

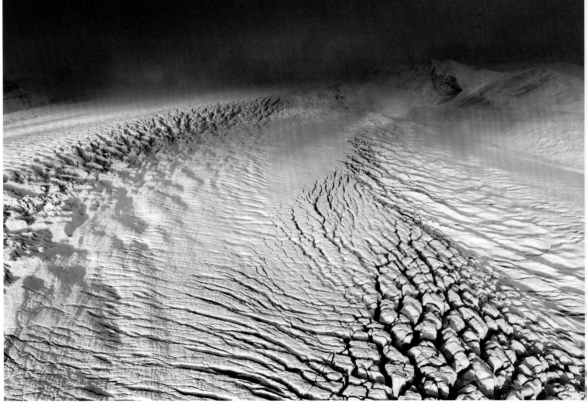

There are candles flickering on every windowsill, an abundance of fluffy cushions and throws and, most surprisingly, a nightly five-course feast of slow food. There's a tendency towards pickled and fermented dishes as well as reindeer provided by one of Svalbard's few remaining trappers, Tommy Sandal, who lives in a cabin with his dogs and has hunted here for over 15 years. We eat fresh sourdough, smoked mackerel mousse, grilled Arctic cod and reindeer every which way before the conversation turns to the unpredictability of ice and whether the Northern Lights can sing. It's easy to forget how far into the wilderness we are until we're shown a scuffed and scratched bottle of red wine, a souvenir from the time a few months ago when a polar bear broke into the storage room and mauled its contents before trying to escape through a window.

After a heavy night's sleep induced by too much cava, we embark on a hike across the broad, flat plain to try and spot a walrus colony, hoping that they won't yet have departed for the season. Led by our guide Ivar and retired husky Borneo, I lose track of how long we spend crunching over ice and stone, the confronting scale shrinking me to Lilliputian dimensions while giving my thoughts space to roam. We eventually reach a dilapidated shipwreck of a cabin – which I'm told would have been a kind of bleak "holiday home" for those at the station needing a break from their colleagues – beyond which a group of 30 or so walruses are huddled together on the shoreline.

We creep towards them while maintaining a respectable distance so as not to disturb them and I forget the slow freezing of my fingers as I watch them roll languorously on to their backs, rear their spindly tusks and effortfully heave themselves into the sea. Such a colony would once have been easy prey for hunters, who would spear the slow-moving land creatures before they could escape into the waves, but today Svalbard's status as a certified Sustainable Destination means that the only capture they risk is through a camera lens. On our way back, we stumble across a small herd of curious reindeer, who with their shaggy winter coats, stocky legs and doleful expressions look rather like white pigs. As with the walruses, it's a shock to encounter wildlife thriving among so much emptiness and I wonder how they survive. ▶ ▶

I awake early the next day and eschew a proposed dip in the ocean as I've forgotten my bikini and don't fancy improvising in the minus-degree cold. Instead I put on every layer I have (nine on top, four on bottom) and waddle to the outhouse to retrieve my bodysuit before we lurch off across the waves in search of glaciers, which cover 60 per cent of Svalbard's landmass. As we crash along while being slapped in the face by spray, a pod of dolphins suddenly erupts from the water and we spot a blow print likely to belong to a blue whale in yet another sign that life is always lurking beneath the surface here. Upon reaching the shockingly turquoise-blue Esmark Glacier we kill the engine and the temperature drops a few degrees further due to the wind bouncing off its surface. The Arctic is known as the "thermometer of the earth" and alongside the Antarctic regulates the temperature of the planet – later, watching a visual of the ice shrinkage in recent decades in Svalbard's museum, it's horrifying to see the speed at which this millennia-old ice is disappearing.

As we ride the final few kilometres into Longyearbyen the first snow of the season starts to fall thick and fast, and by the time we draw in the whole town is blanketed in a layer of white. It appears that winter has arrived just as I'm due to depart. I haven't seen polar bears, whales or the Northern Lights – in many ways, I haven't seen much at all beyond the harsh purity of the landscape – but Svalbard is a place that refutes tick-box tourism. Instead, what I witnessed here was my own insignificance against its age-old vistas, as well as a new community of pioneers dedicated to forging a future based on sustainable tourism rather than exploitation. Although I can't help but roll my eyes when Ben, who stays on a few days longer, excitedly texts me his pictures of his encounters with polar bears and Arctic foxes, I have to accept that Svalbard is a study in patience and letting the land reveal its secrets at its own pace. As Christiane Ritter, a writer who lived in a cabin here in the 1930s, wondered: "Perhaps in the future, man will go into the Arctic in the same way as in Biblical times, man journeyed into the desert in search of the truth".

THE LOWDOWN

Basecamp Explorer's three-day Magic of the Arctic boat safari runs from June to September and is £920 per person (not including a stay at Basecamp Hotel).

To learn more about Basecamp Explorer's series of year-round expeditions including winter ski, snowmobile and sledding experiences go to *basecampexplorer.com/spitsbergen*

For more information about visiting Svalbard go to *visitnorway.com*

Svalbard

Photographer: **MITCH PAYNE**
Stylist: **TONA STELL**

1. M.i.h Jeans Earth Organic Cotton T-Shirt *£85*, **2. Christophe Robin** Regenerating Hair Mask with Rare Prickly-Pear Seed Oil *£57*, **3. Christophe Robin** Regenerating Shampoo with Rare Prickly-Pear Seed Oil *£32.50*, **4. Skinceuticals** Hydrating B5 Masque *£55*, **5. Chilly's Bottles** Bottle in Monochrome Black *£20*, **6. A.P.C.** Morgane Logo Continental Wallet *£164*, **7. Pringle of Scotland** Merino Wool Logo Pants in Red *£650*

8. M.i.h Jeans Lacey Knitted Sweater *£245*, **9. Veja** Hiking Style Sneakers *£164*, **10. Ganni** Callahan Hat *£75*, **11. Jo Loves** Jo by Jo Loves *£115*, **12. Chinti & Parker** Striped Socks *£55*, **13. WEEKDAY** Voyage Rinse Jeans *£40*, **14. Omorovicza** Balancing Moisturiser *£85*, **15. Fujifilm** Instax Square SQ6 Instant Camera *£124.99*

Higher Ground

The photographer Chris Burkard on how travelling to the most remote parts of the planet has helped him understand his own place in the world

Words by **OLIVIA SQUIRE**
Photos by **CHRIS BURKARD**

Despite not having a passport until the age of 20, photographer Chris Burkard has since carved out a (literally) high-flying career for himself as an adventure, surf and conservation photographer, travelling to untouched corners of the globe to document the epic landscapes that thrive there. Drawn to discovering places where humans don't belong – not only because of their raw beauty but also because of the thrill – Burkard is in many ways part of a long line of intrepid explorers. However, rather than looking to exploit, his aim is instead to inspire a sense of awe and responsibility in those who view his work. There's a humbling element to his pictures, where the scale and longevity of each grand horizon underscore the comparative fleetingness of our own lives.

Like so many other photographers and adventurers of his generation, there's a touch of the activist to Burkard. Having shot all over the world, his projects in Iceland, the Faroe Islands and most recently in Alaska's Aleutian Islands with Conservation International have inspired an Instagram following of over three million and have seen him speak on the TED stage. We pin him down from his home in California to discuss storytelling, the dangers of "bucket-listing" and inciting change by capturing the world's wildest enclaves. ▶ ▶

HAWAII

Tell us how you began your career as a photographer.

I'm from a small town three-and-a-half hours north of LA. It was the gateway to Big Sur and I grew up surfing, so I'm a real by-product of the open expanses of that early environment. Initially photography was the perfect form of expression for me to document my surfer friends, but later it dawned on me that it could also be my ticket out. At first, I just wanted to get some stamps in my passport and a paycheck, but after a certain point it became more of a calling and led me to places where I was really forced to give myself to the craft. There was never a big break though – it's always been a hustle. I did a series of internships before I applied for a grant that I spent on a 50-day road trip of California's coast which turned into my first book, The California Surf Project – my love letter to California and still one of the best-selling surf books out there. It really changed me and set me down the path of what I wanted to create – meaningful projects that require a lot of myself.

How did you decide what kind of stories you wanted to tell?

The concept of being a storyteller is definitely something that has evolved. The California road trip helped to define the style of my work, partially because a book makes you think long term. After a few years I found myself travelling to incredible places like Nicaragua and Costa Rica for surf magazines but although this was sometimes fulfilling, it was often really boring as I felt I was just travelling in the footsteps of others. Although surf has remained a key part of my work, I've since moved towards seeking out remote, wild places such as Greenland, Iceland, Norway and Russia. The purity of their landscapes drew me in – I knew I could find stories there that hadn't been told before.

How do you decide on your next destination?

I have a laundry list of really remote locations I want to get to based on years of research scrolling through Google Earth and contacting whoever's been there, even if it's a random fisherman. However, I actually thrive on going back to places where I've been before. When I hear people say that everything's been seen and done somewhere, I don't believe them. Iceland is a favourite of mine – I've been 31 times. Everyone is stuck in this same stretch of six-hour southern coast, but there are places there that are totally isolated if you get off the well-trodden path and allow yourself to be caught off-guard. Even though it's now on everyone's radar, the thing that keeps me going back is that my understanding of the country drives me to new locations within and also allows me to become involved on a deeper level. I've been working alongside the Icelandic government's environmental branch, for example, to help create a national park in the interior of the country.

One of your recent significant projects was with Conservation International documenting the remote Aleutian Islands in Alaska. Why did you choose them as a subject?

I'd previously spent some time there as part of a trip for a magazine and it blew my mind. The region is not only part of a "ring of fire" of active volcanoes but also a marine reserve with a strong protection order. The land is so pristine as to be uninhabitable and flying over the volcanoes is really dangerous, so there's no observation technology there. I wanted to document it from the land and I'm hoping to go back within the next year, ideally working with Alaska's volcanologist society. Conservation International is a great partner because it's well-known, really smart and has lots of connections. We went back and forth about which location to shoot – I wanted to educate people about something that is under protection. Instilling a sense of wonder and awe is just as important as being on the front lines of preventing environmental destruction.

What is the relationship between photography and activism?

Essentially the more time you spend in wild places, the more you want to protect them. You can talk until your nose bleeds to people in rural Africa about glaciers, for example, but until they see it they won't be moved. How can we expect change to occur in any capacity unless we show people why they should care? Photography is a step towards this – it incites us to be excited. People travel because of imagery to experience things they would never have otherwise. Conservation is still something I'm just beginning to understand, but we all have a responsibility to engage with the issues that we're facing. I'd be doing myself and the destinations I visit a disservice if I didn't try and learn from them and immerse myself in their problems. I get requests to go to places all the time, but I try to explain that instead of jumping on the bandwagon, it's better to be passionate and make a real difference in one campaign. I aim to use my images to inspire others and allow them to form their own opinions, because that's what incites real change – not being bombarded with information and being told what not to do.

What have your travels taught you?

Travel is a drug and going to new places incites all the same feelings. We're excited, scared, our endorphins are running. However, everywhere I go, I quickly realise that there's a life of exploration in each place. We need to get away from the mentality of ticking things off a list. Once you begin to understand that there are deeper issues at stake, travel becomes what you dream about – I still frequently dream of Iceland and want to make sure my images are benefitting the country. I hope that my work will be around a lot longer than I am.

ALEUTIAN ISLANDS

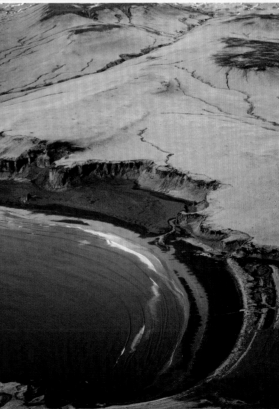

ICELAND

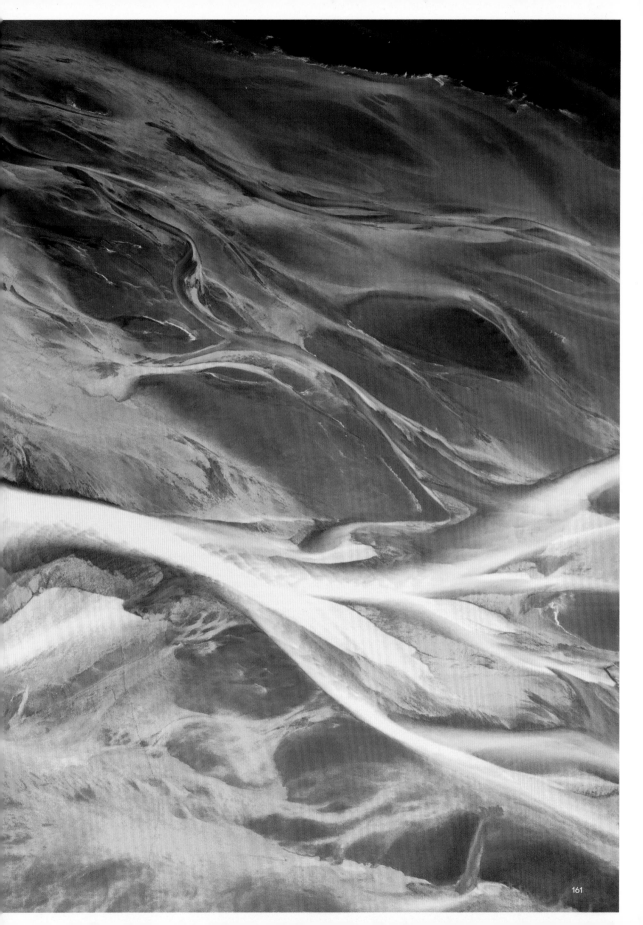

ALEUTIAN ISLANDS

PHOTOS BY CHRIS BURKARD/MASSIF

ICELAND

WISH YOU WERE HERE
with

Captain Jon McBride

Jon McBride is a former NASA astronaut who has logged almost 200 hours among the stars. Although he is now more commonly found at the Kennedy Space Center Visitor Complex in Florida, here he reflects on his time in orbit with a missive from outer space.

Dear SUITCASE,

After launch, my job as pilot is to power down everything upfront, move to the aft and set up for on-orbit operations. When I hit the button to open the payload bay doors, I get tears in my eyes and a swelling in my chest thinking about how lucky I am to get to experience the amazing view of Earth from up here. Not much time to sit and watch the world go by, though. There's work to do during our eight-day mission, including objectives like a satellite launch and high-tech observations of the Earth. The time will pass quickly and before I know it, we'll be landing home. For now, though, there's still lots to explore...

Captain Jon McBride